Observing Children and Families

Beyond the Surface

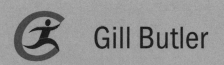
Gill Butler

First published in 2015 by Critical Publishing Ltd

British Library Cataloguing in Publication Data
A CIP record for this book is available from the British Library

ISBN: 978-1-910391-62-4

This book is also available in the following e-book formats:

MOBI ISBN: 978-1-910391-63-1
EPUB ISBN: 978-1-910391-64-8
Adobe e-book ISBN: 978-1-910391-65-5

The rights of Gill Butler and Pia Parry be identified as the Authors of this work have been asserted by them in accordance with the Copyright, Design and Patents Act 1988.

Cover and text design by Greensplash Limited
Project Management by Out of House Publishing
Printed and bound in Great Britain by TJ International

Critical Publishing
152 Chester Road
Northwich
CW8 4AL
www.criticalpublishing.com

MIX
Paper from
responsible sources
FSC
www.fsc.org   FSC® C013056

Contents

Figures

Meet the authors

Gill Butler is an Emeritus Research Fellow at the University of Chichester. She has worked in a variety of statutory and voluntary social work settings, which have included practising as a children's guardian for many years while also teaching at the University of Chichester in the social work department. She was head of social studies programmes and as deputy dean had particular responsibility for learning and teaching. Her practice and thinking is also informed by her role as a trustee of a domestic abuse charity, as well as her personal experience as a mother and grandmother.

Pia Parry is Head of Department for Childhood, Social Work and Social Care at the University of Chichester. Her professional background in therapeutic work with young children and their families has advanced her observational practice and interest in research in this field.

Acknowledgements

Over the years I have been very fortunate to work with many wonderful colleagues and students at Chichester, from whom I have learned a great deal. Special thanks go to former students and practitioners who generously gave their time to share their experiences of using observation: Anita Ademah, Emily Beirne, Jenny Brennan, Jo Green, Lissi Holstad, Sian Kemp, Sara Lee, Donna Price, Sue Ridgewell, Hazel Rumsey and Mohammed Taha, and to Chris Smethurst who facilitated this process.

The children who have been observed are at the heart of this book, so I am greatly indebted to them. My thanks to all the children and their carers for allowing us a window into their lives.

While writing this book I have received much encouragement, support and helpful feedback. I would especially like to thank Pia Parry, Jean Duncombe and Jan Spafford, who has also contributed excerpts from her observations, for reading and commenting on earlier drafts of the book.

Lastly, but by no means least, my thanks to John for his endless support and encouragement, and to my children, particularly Sophie, for her help and skills in drawing diagrams, and my grandchildren, for being themselves!

Introduction

This book in part reflects my own journey in learning about observation. When I was first invited to participate in an observation seminar group facilitated by Gillian Miles of the Tavistock Institute in the late 1990s, it triggered an anxiety in me that perhaps there was rather more to observing than I had hitherto realised, despite being an experienced social work practitioner. The ensuing opportunity to observe a young child over the course of a year resulted in a unique and rich learning experience for me, where I came to realise that, rather like the fictional Dr Watson who accompanied Sherlock Holmes, I could *see*, but on a daily basis I failed to *observe*, or understand, much of what was actually in front of me (Conan Doyle 1892). My observation was perhaps more akin to a surface glance to confirm or disprove my expectations about what I expected to see, based on my own experience. I might know some of what was happening, but had I understood the meaning of what I was observing? How carefully had I focused my attention on the finer details of what was there, but was not on my immediate agenda? Did I think about what I was seeing, or was my thinking driven by what I had been told?

The journey to improving my observation skills has at times been difficult, but the benefits have made this very worthwhile. Greater awareness of what I bring as a practitioner has resulted in a deeper understanding of what is entailed in observation and greater confidence that I am a little closer to understanding the experience of children and young people. Maintaining effective observational skills is an ongoing struggle and the battle can easily be lost when life is difficult, personally or professionally.

Since undertaking my training in observation I have taught observation skills to multi-disciplinary groups at post-qualifying levels and to final-year social work students on the undergraduate qualifying social work programme. This book is intended to be a helpful, practical source of support for any student or practitioner seeking to develop their skills or deepen their understanding of observation. While it has primarily been written for those working in social work, it may also be useful for a wider range of professionals working with children and their families, hence the term 'practitioners' will be used predominantly throughout the book. It is designed to enable you to explore your understanding of the concept of observation and to enrich your skills as an observer. It will attempt to explain the unique insights that holistic, experiential observation can bring to practice with children and families and will help you to further develop your own approach to incorporating observation in your practice. It also provides a range of examples from practitioners who use observation in their practice.

Observation

The importance of observation in work with children and families is highlighted in the *Framework for the Assessment of Children and Families* (Department of Health 2000), and the Munro review called for practitioners to have '*well developed skills in observation*' (Munro 2011: 6.35). These documents reflect an assumption that observation is a core component of social work practice, and that practitioners need to be good at it. However, there has been very little discussion of what is meant by observation, of how to go about it, of how skills in observing can be developed, or of what factors might make observing challenging. Neither are there any explicit references to observation within the HCPC *Standards of Proficiency* (Health Care Professions Council 2012) or the College of Social Work *Professional Capabilities Framework* (College of Social Work 2012), although the ability to observe is arguably implicit in the following capabilities.

- *Gather information so as to inform judgement for interventions in more complex situations and in response to challenge.*
- *Use assessment procedures discerningly so as to inform judgement.*
- *Develop a range of interventions; use them effectively and evaluate them in practice.*
- *Expand intervention methods and demonstrate expertise in one or more specific methods relevant to your setting.*

Skills in observation will also support the development of skills required in the critical reflection and analysis domain.

- *Routinely and efficiently apply critical reflection and analysis to increasingly complex cases.*
- *Ensure hypotheses and options are reviewed to inform judgement and decision-making.*
- *Start to provide professional opinion.*

It might be assumed that there is so little discussion about observation because it is not needed and it is a straightforward task; we all know how to do it well and share a common understanding of what is entailed. However, it is far from straightforward. Social conventions are designed to diminish conflict and thus tend to obscure truth and accuracy, so what we are presented with may consciously or unconsciously be designed to conceal the truth (Hammond 2007: 38). According to Hammond this is a defence mechanism that exists in all human interactions, but will clearly be to the fore when working with children and families in contexts where there is uncertainty and anxiety about the consequences of the truth being revealed. What practitioners are being told may often be at odds with what they are observing, and what is being selected for a practitioner to observe may have been carefully set up or chosen by those whom we are observing.

It is also apparent that both on an individual and on a professional level there are different understandings of and approaches to observation which will be explored, enabling you to develop approaches to observation that are best suited to the context and needs of the work that you are engaged in.

What do we mean by observation?

Most of us carry an unconscious understanding of what it means to observe, shaped by our personal experiences and culture, which may then be modified by our professional frame of reference as well as the purpose of the observation. Hence, before we begin any observation we have a 'view' about what we will see, which then informs what we observe.

Within this book 'child observation' refers to the process of giving our total, focused attention to the child, to learning about the child, directly from them, from their appearance, their movements, the sounds they make, their expressions, their actions, their play, their use of language, their interaction with others, their interaction with their environment and every facet of their lived experience. This approach is best described as experiential and holistic. It entails developing a way of being open, staying with uncertainty and making use of our reactions and responses as part of a process of developing an understanding of what we are seeing (Trowell and Miles 1991). It is a tool and a stepping stone to reaching an understanding of the child's lived experience.

The word 'children' will be used to include babies and young people up to the age of 18 (in accordance with the definitions used in The United Nations Convention on the Rights of the Child (UNCRC) and the Children Act 1989). However, there will be some specific references to babies and young people when there are issues that need to be considered separately. The main focus in the book is on observing children, as without a clear focus they can so easily slip from our sight. However, children also need to be understood within the wider social and economic context that they live in, so it is also important to observe their interactions with their families, carers and, ideally, teachers and friends, as well as recognising the impact of the physical environment. The approach to observation that will be explored can be seen as relevant in all these contexts and across the lifespan, if adapted with sensitivity to the context and wishes of those being observed.

In Chapter 1 we will briefly explore contemporary understandings of what it means to be a child in the United Kingdom in the twenty-first century. Our ideas about children shape our views about them and inform the ways in which we choose to spend time with them. They impact on how we interpret what we observe when we are with children. This chapter will explore these ideas and provide a rationale for the need to rethink how we see children in the twenty-first century in the United Kingdom. The chapter will then consider the findings of some child death inquiries that illustrate some of the difficulties in seeing, thinking about and developing an understanding of children's experience.

Chapter 2 describes a range of approaches to observation that are commonly used in work with children and their families in the UK, noting the preference for particular approaches in different professional settings. It will address the debates about objectivity and the role of observers as non-participants or participants. The experiential, holistic approach that we have used at Chichester, based on the Tavistock method, will be explored more fully and is presented as being of particular relevance for social workers. Vignettes will be used to demonstrate the application of the approaches with supporting activities to encourage reflection on their relative advantages and disadvantages.

Chapter 3 is designed to support the development of the skills needed to develop an observational stance. A series of activities has been designed to help observers through each stage of the process, including preparing themselves to observe effectively and negotiating their role with those whom they wish to observe. A sample agreement form is included as well as discussion of the issues relating to consent in relation both to the child and to any adults who may be observed. Approaches to recording, reflection and developing an understanding of what has been observed are discussed, alongside an emphasis on a transparent approach to practice that requires openness in sharing what has been observed with those who have been observed. This chapter is accompanied by activities that replicate typical issues that are explored in seminar groups.

Chapter 4 addresses some of the key issues that practitioners need to consider in any practice setting, including ones where they will be observing; an appreciation of issues related to identity, power and difference are central to all direct work with children and families. The chapter then provides examples of the way in which observation may make a valuable contribution to practice. While some of the suggestions come from published articles, most were provided by former students on qualifying and post-qualifying courses. They were invited to participate in focus groups or individual interviews to talk about their views on observation and to provide examples of how they had used observation in their practice. In some cases managers passed the invitation on to others who were in direct practice, hence not all the respondents were former Chichester students. They provided an interesting range of examples of the use of observation, primarily in the context of assessing children and families, but some examples illustrate the potential for observation to have a therapeutic impact in interventions with children and families.[1]

Chapter 5 highlights the relevance of key theoretical concepts and research as the basis for reflecting, analysing and making sense of what has been observed. Social work practice is enriched by thinking from a wide range of disciplines, although the perceived value of these within the profession has varied over time, depending on the prevailing political and ideological discourses in social work. The selection of particular theoretical concepts necessarily reflects my personal biases as well as the revival of interest within social work in relationship-based approaches to practice.

The chapter includes an introduction to some of the recent thinking on the process of exercising judgement, enabled by developments in neuroscience and cognitive psychology. Insights

---

[1] All examples have been anonymised and some details changed to ensure that any identifying details have been removed or altered.

are provided from psychoanalytic thinking, relating to transference and containment, as well as from theory that may be more familiar to those working with children and families, such as attachment and separation. These will be discussed with reference to practice examples to help you to use research and theory to inform your thinking about practice. In this chapter the problematic nature of the concepts of developmental progress, norms and milestones, discussed in Chapter 2, is recognised, but it will be argued that tools based on these concepts may also be of value if used with a critical awareness of their limitations.

Learning activities

Each chapter is accompanied by reflective activities and case studies which practitioners can relate to their own practice. It is, however, recognised that skills cannot be developed by simply reading a book. Practice, reflection and ideally practice discussions are needed to support the development of skills. As part of the development of your professionalism you are encouraged to make use of the activities and seek the support of your colleagues to explore your thinking.

A cautionary note

Arguably the most profound thing that I learned from my participation in a year-long child-observation seminar group, where each of us had undertaken an extended observation of a young child, was that the child whom each of us presented to the seminar group reflected very closely the preoccupations and worries in our own lives, arguably reflecting these more closely than the reality of the lived experience of the children whom we had observed. We had presented our own insecurities, boundary issues or façade that all was well. We had somehow made these issues a core part of our understanding of the child. The subsequent process of reflection in the context of theoretical frameworks enabled us to recognise these limitations and see beyond our initial surface views. My experience was echoed by Rosie King (2002), who was '*struck by the way the children observed seemed to mirror the personality and preoccupations of the observer*' when she participated in a similar observation seminar group.

The difficulty of trying to see beyond the limits of our own experience emerges as a core issue that is worth holding in mind as you read the book and reflect on your own practice.

References

College of Social Work (2012) *Professional Capabilities Framework.* London: College of Social Work, www.tcsw.org.uk/ProfessionalCapabilitiesFramework/ (accessed 13 July 2015).

Conan Doyle, A (1892) *The Adventures of Sherlock Holmes.* London: George Newnes.

Department of Health (2000) *Framework for the Assessment of Children in Need and Their Families.* London: Stationery Office, http://webarchive.nationalarchives.gov.uk/ (accessed 13 July 2015).

Hammond, K (2007) *Beyond Rationality: The Search for Wisdom in a Troubled Time.* New York: Oxford University Press.

Health Care Professions Council (2012) *Standards of Proficiency for Social Workers*, www.hpc-uk.org/assets/documents/10003B08Standardsofproficiency-SocialworkersinEngland.pdf (accessed 13 July 2015).

King, R (2002) The Experience of Undertaking Child Observation as Part of the PQ Award in Child Care. *Journal of Social Work Practice*, 16: 213–21.

Monro, E (2011) *Monro Review of Child Protection: Interim Report: The Child's Journey*. DfE.00010-2011. London.

Trowell, J and Miles, G (1991) The Contribution of Observation Training to Professional Development in Social Work. *Journal of Social Work Practice*, 5(1): 51–60.

1 Seen, but not seen and not heard

Objectives

- To explore current perceptions of children in the UK and explore the impact that these may have on practice with children and their families and carers.

- To consider the difficulties in seeing and hearing children, as revealed through official inquiries into child deaths, drawing on findings from research, government inquiries and Serious Case Reviews, from Maria Colwell to Daniel Pelka.

- To reflect on the persistence of the difficulties in seeing and hearing children.

Introduction

I don't bother observing babies: there's nothing to see.
I can't think of anything more boring.

Comments like these were made to me on a number of occasions when I was practising as a children's guardian and often reflect the assumptions made by some students and practitioners, who think that observing babies will not be very worthwhile. In practice we have found that when social work students are asked to find a child to observe between 0 and 5 years old, they very rarely choose to observe young babies. While the reasons given are usually practical, they may be seen as the extreme end of ambivalent feelings about spending time with infants, children and young people. This chapter will help us to begin to understand some of the reasons why this may be difficult and will illustrate the persistence of the difficulties in seeing and understanding children's experience.

Activity

When someone says 'children', what are the first ten words that come to mind?

Write them down.

Looking at those words, what do they reflect in terms of your views about children?

Repeat the exercise, but this time with the word 'babies'.

COMMENT

It can be difficult to come up with ten words, but your list may have included words that reflect children's vulnerability, or maybe you have a different view, that emphasises children's competence and abilities. The way that we think about children and babies has a very significant impact on what we see when we are with them and whether we choose to spend time with them. It affects how we interpret their actions and the actions of those caring for them. Changing views about whether children are 'innocent' or understand concepts of good and bad can be illustrated historically by changes in attitudes towards criminal activity and the age at which children can be held accountable for their actions.

Cunningham (2006: 13) found that a seven-year-old child could be hanged for theft in the eighteenth century, whereas in the tenth century there was a debate about increasing the age of responsibility from twelve to fifteen (Cunningham 2006: 24). Currently children are held to be criminally responsible in England, Wales and Northern Ireland at the age of ten. In Scotland the age of criminal responsibility is eight, but until the age of 12 children are referred to a social worker and Children's Hearing rather than being prosecuted (www.nspcc.org.uk). The age of criminal responsibility in the UK is therefore much lower than in other countries in the European Union, where for example it is 15 in Denmark and 16 in Spain.

Activity

At what age do you think children should be held criminally responsible for their actions?

How would you justify this?

What does this tell you about your perception of children?

Perceptions of children

The notion of childhood as something that is other than and different to adulthood is comparatively recent. Hendrick (2005: 31) argues that there are four influential constructions of children and young people in Britain:

* **children as victims**, highly vulnerable and in need of protection (abused children);

* **children as incomplete adults**, human *becomings* (Qvortrup 1994);

* **children as a threat** to social order (moral outrage at young offenders);

* **children as redemptive**, an investment against an uncertain future: this view of children and young people emphasises their importance to society in the future.

All of these perceptions can present potential blocks to feeling that there is something to be learned from spending time with children and that it is worthwhile engaging with their lived experience. The first two are particularly problematic and relevant to practitioners, so these will be explored more fully below.

Children as victims

Few things provoke a stronger public outcry than the death of children at the hands of 'strangers', paedophiles or sometimes even those who care for them. Although the number of such deaths is relatively small there is usually widespread publicity, a desire to attribute blame and a cry for something to be done to reduce risks, so ensuring that children are more effectively protected in the future. While the portrayal of children as victims, who are vulnerable and often unable to protect themselves, is in such instances entirely appropriate, it has a wider impact on perceptions of children generally. The view of children as dependent, helpless and in need of adult protection has contributed to increasingly limited opportunities for children to exercise appropriate independence in late twentieth century Britain (Alderson 2000). Changes in the environment are also highlighted by Alderson as further contributing to the virtual imprisonment of children in their own homes. Hence, while in 1971 80 per cent of British school children aged seven to eight went to school on their own, by 1990 only 9 per cent did so (Hillman, Adams and Whiteleg, cited in Alderson 2000: 99). Lansdown (1995) has drawn helpful distinctions between children's inherent dependence and that which is *structured* by the society that they live in.

Similarly, attitudes to children working have also changed, so within the framework of the law there is now a '*protectionist discourse*' (James, Jenks and Prout 1998) that regards the employment of young children as intrinsically problematic. Cunningham suggests that this has had a problematic impact:

> So fixated are we on giving our children a long and happy childhood that we downplay their abilities and their resilience. To think of children as potential victims in need of protection is a very modern outlook, and it probably does no-one a service.
>
> (Cunningham 2006: 245)

My tendency to view children in this way was vividly illustrated when I was visiting South Africa some years ago. I saw a young girl, at most six years old, carrying a baby (approximately 9–12 months) on her back, purposefully making her way along and across a busy road. She did this carefully and competently. The baby on her back had his arms curled around her; he looked chubby and alert. The image has always stayed in my mind, as it was a sight that did not fit with my view of children's competence and the level of responsibility that they should be afforded.

Activity

Do you agree with Cunningham's view, stated above, that it is unhelpful to see children as potential victims? Compile a list of the possible advantages and disadvantages.

COMMENT

Constraining children's freedom in order to prevent them from becoming possible victims is usually justified on the basis that it is for their long-term good and ensures their safety. However, if the same reasoning is applied to all people, it is likely that many activities that adults enjoy engaging in (motor sports, bungee jumping) would be regarded as unacceptable. Similar debates also arise in relation to older people who may be physically or mentally frail.

Children as incomplete adults, or as *'human becomings'* (Qvortrup 1994)

Seeing childhood as a transient state to be passed through, en route to becoming a fully fledged member of the human race, renders it something of less value than mature adulthood. Children are often considered to be too young to be able to comment, or contribute to discussions, even where the subject matter directly affects them. Their incomplete understanding and inexperience has been used to justify not giving children and young people a voice in democratic processes until the age of 18 in the UK, although interestingly when it is politically expedient, this can change: the voting age was reduced to 16 in Scotland to enable young people to participate in the 2014 referendum on Scottish independence.

The view of children as incomplete is subtly reinforced through developmental psychology, which provides a highly influential framework for professionals' understanding of children. Hence it has been widely accepted that children develop increasing ability according to certain established stages that are strongly related to age. While such frameworks can be helpful (as discussed in Chapter 4) they may also be problematic. Mayall (1996) and James, Jenks and Prout (1998: 17–19) draw attention to the established critiques of Piaget, which have substantially undermined his findings. Their critiques highlight the dangers in:

*   decontextualising our understanding of children;

*   underestimating their competence;

*   seeing them as passive recipients of socialisation processes.

Furthermore Piaget's early experiments seeking to identify children's cognitive abilities treated children as laboratory objects, to be classified according to their developmental stage, which was in turn linked to a specified age. His notion of the natural child, passing through stages to reach maturity, has persisted, and despite the recognition of the need for more flexible and interactionist perspectives, developmental frameworks continue to inform the way that health and social care professionals view children. It could be argued that the persistence of a decontextualised understanding of children is politically convenient within a neoliberal ideology, as the concentrated focus on the child in isolation from their family and environment removes the need to look at the impact of poverty, poor housing and deprivation (Featherstone 2014: 2).

These difficulties can create a tendency to limit our gaze, viewing children in relation to their level of conformity, or deviance from the framework, as an object of study, rather than a unique human being with individual qualities and abilities. Mayall (2002: 21) points out that:

> *[C]hildren are social actors; that is they take part in family relationships from the word go; they express their wishes, demonstrate strong attachments, jealousy and delight, seek justice.*

If children are not recognised as social actors, it arguably reduces the need to engage with them, or to spend time with them trying to understand their subjective reality (Hill and Tisdell 1997). It also reduces the possibility of children being able to exercise *agency*. The term *agency* is used by sociologists to refer to the ability of a person to make a difference to interactions and decisions. Within the Children Act (1989), which provides the current framework for safeguarding and promoting the welfare of children, there is a clear expectation that children are recognised as social actors and arguably as having agency, as in making any decision about the welfare of a child, courts are required to have particular regard to

> *the ascertainable wishes and feelings of the child concerned (considered in the light of his age and understanding).*
>
> (Children Act 1989 Part 1.1.3 a)

A further difficulty identified by Skolnick (Mayall 1996: 46) is that implicit in the notion of stages of development must be the notion that there is a final stage, adulthood, when development is complete and full citizenship attained. Inevitably this raises the question as to when in adulthood our development can be said to be complete – at 20, or 40, or 60, or perhaps when we have children? Presumably then some adults must be described as developmentally immature; should they therefore be excluded from full participation in society? Should adults with dementia or mental health issues therefore be excluded?

Clearly this line of thinking is dangerous, as we accept that our development as adults is a slow, evolutionary process, influenced by interactions with those around us, as well as our environment, and that *regardless of our development or competence* we all have a right to be heard, to exercise agency and to participate. It is also deeply disturbing, as this is precisely the line of thinking that has so often been used by the powerful to exclude other less powerful members of society (women, black people and people with disabilities) from full participation. It is important to recognise the parallels in the exclusion of children from participation, as they also have a minority status. Many of the arguments used to negate the contribution of children, such as *'they will only say what they think you want to hear'*, are equally true for adults, particularly where there may be consequences in relation to revealing information that the speaker fears may result in a course of action that is unwelcome. What this does mean is that we should always take time to consider the spoken word in the context of other messages conveyed non-verbally and received through our senses.

Further challenges to established ways of viewing children are posed by Bluebond-Langner and Alderson's research, with seriously ill children, cited in Alderson (2000). They found that children's understanding was more closely related to experience than to age. Alderson (2000) explored the possibility of actively consulting very young children on a range of issues. She found that giving sufficient information in appropriate ways enabled children to participate.

Activity

Write down how you would feel if you were asked to observe a child aged three for one hour, on three occasions.

What does this tell you about you feel about spending time with young children? How would this be different with a baby, or a young person?

COMMENT

The way in which you may have responded to this task will in part be determined by your own personal experience of being with babies and children of different ages. However, it will also be shaped by the wider social and cultural understandings of childhood and any theories that have been relied upon to explain children's development. It is therefore important to think critically about the impact of established norms on our understanding of children and to be aware of the way these may constrain our view, particularly in relation to children's competence (Daniel and Ivatts 1998).

How do these perceptions of children impact on the practice of social workers?

The initial part of this chapter has focused on the way in which childhood and children's lives are constructed and given meaning within the UK today. It has been suggested that this contributes to a view that limits the understanding of childhood as being worthwhile in its own right and of children as competent social actors.

If the *present* of childhood is not seen as of value, inevitably the actual *presence* of children is less likely to be seen as necessary. It may then be difficult for hard-pressed practitioners to justify spending their limited time with children. As children become less visible, what may also be missed is the capacity of the child to contribute to an understanding of their experience, albeit with the support of the social worker, because their competence and experience is not recognised.

If as practitioners we are uncertain about the priority to be accorded to gaining information directly from children who have meaningful expressive language, we may find it even more difficult to prioritise spending time with children who do not have expressive language, either because of their age, developmental delay, disability or because English is not their first language.

Child death inquiries

Why look at child death inquiries?

We have considered some current perceptions of children that may impact on practice. The next section will provide some brief summaries of child death reviews, selected from each decade in the last 40 years. They illustrate some of the consistent difficulties that arise in seeing beyond the surface of what is presented, which also emerge in the overview studies of Serious Case Reviews (Brandon et al 2012).

However, before turning to these it is important to contextualise them. In 2009–10, of the 11 million children in England, 38,400 were the subject of a child protection plan (Brandon et al 2012). They estimate that there were approximately 85 violent and maltreatment-related child (0–17) deaths in that year. Of those, only 10 per cent had a child protection plan in place, a decrease of 6 per cent from the previous two-year period. This suggests that many of the children who died had not previously been recognised as high risk, so perhaps were less well known to social workers.

Pritchard and Williams (2010), using data from the World Health Organization (WHO) between 1974 and 2006, found that deaths in England and Wales that could be attributed to child abuse decreased significantly, compared to deaths from other causes during that time. They contrasted this with findings in other countries, notably the USA, where the reverse was true. It could therefore be argued that given the relative success of statutory services in intervening effectively in the lives of so many vulnerable children, it is inappropriate to focus on the very small number of children each year who die as a result of negligent or abusive behaviour by their parents.

However, given the often extreme suffering of the children concerned, it can also be argued that it is difficult to understand why no one was able to see and appreciate the seriousness of what was happening, despite some involvement in most cases of a number of statutory services, including health, education and social work. Thus, if some of the most vulnerable children are not seen or heard, it may be reasonable to assume that similar difficulties are occurring for other children who are in need and are similarly not understood.

Activity

> *When looking at the following summaries, consider how far the perceptions of children outlined above may have affected the practice of the professionals with whom the children came into contact.*
>
> *Can you identify any other themes or issues?*

1973: Maria Colwell died, aged seven years

Maria was the youngest of five children. Her father, who had left shortly after her birth, died when she was four months old. Her mother was unable to cope and so Maria went to live with her aunt, while the other four children were received into care. In June 1966 at the age of 15 months she was briefly removed by her mother from the care of her aunt and placed with another woman, who was deemed by social services to be unsuitable. She was then returned to the care of her aunt, but it was recognised that this was not a permanent solution. It is important when reflecting on these events to recognise that the legal framework was different and that the clear expectation was that children should be returned to a parent as long as they were considered to be a 'fit person'.

By 1970 Maria's mother, having formed a new relationship and had another three children, wanted Maria back. There was consequently a great deal of social work involvement with the family. Maria made her resistance to returning to her birth mother (Pauline Kepple) and step-father very clear to her social worker, who witnessed her distress. On one occasion the social worker had to abandon an attempt to collect Maria and take her to visit her mother because she was so distressed. On another occasion, the report of the Committee of Inquiry states that:

> *Maria continued to cry and said she wanted to go back to 'mummy and daddy Cooper' and begged not to be sent back to Pauline. When Mrs Kepple appeared to claim her Maria cringed, according to Mrs Shirley (another aunt).*
>
> (DHSS 1974: 29)

The social worker '*thought she calmed down quite well and allowed herself to be taken home where she was quite bright and chatty*'. On another occasion the social worker described Maria as '*happy but subdued*'.

These must also have been very difficult and distressing experiences for the social worker trying to manage a planned returned home which was believed to be inevitable and, in the long term, best for Maria. If it had been possible for the social worker to think about her experiences with Maria, and if these experiences were thought about in conjunction with the subsequent complaints from neighbours who saw her bruises, heard her screams and described her as looking skeletal, perhaps the level of concern about Maria's well-being would have been greater. What is interesting is that despite the social worker 'seeing' this, it did not raise sufficient concern to sway social services from the view that this course of action was appropriate. Maria's distress was in fact interpreted as an expression of the trauma and insecurity that she had previously experienced through her earlier separation, initially from her mother and subsequently from her aunt. It is not clear whether any attempts were made to understand Maria's experience or to talk to her or her step-siblings, but the majority report is critical of the failure of the key social workers to communicate directly with Maria and recommended that in such circumstances social workers need to see the child alone and need to be aware of the child's communication with others, for example teachers, to supplement the direct communication with the child (DHSS 1974: 37, 76–78).

When Maria died she weighed only 16.5 kilograms, some 2.5 kilograms below the 2nd centile[1] and 6.5 kilograms below the 25th centile, which she might reasonably have attained given her birth weight. She had been seen by her social worker and her GP (who noted her silence) in the last month of her life. By that time she had given up her earlier vocal protests, which had been ignored and reinterpreted in the light of professional knowledge and understanding. Thoughtful observation of her slender physique, her injuries and her behaviour,

---

[1] Centile charts plot the typical growth patterns of all children, providing a helpful reference point for understanding whether a child's physical development is within the expected range. Significant deviations from the expected range should always prompt further inquiries. If a child's height is on the 25th centile, this means that for every 100 children of that age, 25 would be expected to be shorter and 74 taller. Similarly a weight between the 0.4th centile and 2nd centile indicates that around 99 per cent of children of the same age would be heavier than this.

combined with listening to her expressed communication, should have prompted greater anxiety about her experience and well-being. As we will see, this difficulty in putting pieces of the picture together is a consistent theme when professionals are faced with such disturbing evidence.

1984: Jasmine Beckford died, aged four years

Jasmine's mother, Beverley Lorrington, began living with Maurice Beckford (Jasmine's step-father) when she was pregnant with Jasmine. There were concerns about Jasmine's development from the time of her birth. Beverley and Maurice then had a child together. In September 1981, when Jasmine's younger sister was three months old, both children were admitted to hospital with non-accidental injuries and were made the subjects of interim Care Orders, followed by full Care Orders. The children were placed with foster parents, but in accordance with the expressed views of the magistrates, they were later returned home to their parents. Social services were thus involved in supervising Care Orders for three years before Jasmine's death.

In her evidence to the inquiry into Jasmine's death, her social worker said that 'the family obviously loved the children'. The basis for this comment appears to have been what she was told by the parents, rather than any other source of evidence. She acknowledged that she had only seen Jasmine once in ten months, as she had believed the parents' explanations of why Jasmine was not present. The inquiry criticised the social workers for focusing on the parents and concluded that:

> Throughout the three years of social work with the Beckfords, Ms Walstrom totally misconceived her role as the fieldworker enforcing Care Orders in respect of two very young children at risk. Her gaze focused on Beverley Lorrington and Morris Beckford; she averted her eyes from the children to be aware of them only as and when they were with their parents, hardly even to observe their development, and never to communicate with Jasmine on her own.

(Blom-Cooper 1985: 293)

When she died Jasmine weighed only 10.5 kilograms, although her height at death placed her on the 25th centile of children, hence her weight should have been approximately 16 kilograms. She had forty injuries to her face and body – her ribs were broken and she had ulcers, burns and cuts to her leg. Sadly neither her low weight nor the catalogue of injuries inflicted on her was seen and understood.

1993: Paul[2] died, aged 15 months

Paul was the youngest of seven children. There had been 15 years of involvement by agencies including health, social services, education, probation, housing and the police. Many of the social work concerns had related to poor hygiene, and interventions were designed to provide practical support, equipment and short-term payments to avert crises due to a shortage of money. However, in the years preceding Paul's birth there was increasing evidence of

---

[2] Paul's full name was not released for publication, so helping to protect the identities of his siblings.

the family's inability to care for the children, demonstrated in relation to the older children, as well as the diagnosis of developmental delay and failure to thrive in the sibling next to Paul in chronological age. At Paul's eight-month developmental assessment, he was recorded as unable to sit up. The inquiry found that the perception of the professionals was that the family could cope, if they were given the right help. The fixed view included a perception that the children were happy, but no evidence is provided to support this, and indeed the acute embarrassment suffered by the older children as a result of their dirtiness clearly made engagement with peers very difficult. As a result, there was no attempt to understand what life was like for the children in the household. The inquiry considered that the neglect by Paul's parents was paralleled by Paul's absence from the records of the professionals and their failure to recognise what was happening to his older siblings. The inquiry states:

> We cannot stress too highly how important it is that there is a clear methodology which allows for skilled, creative discussions with children and young people. **They are living the experience and can give a more accurate picture of what life is like in a family than any assessment made by a professional**.
>
> (Bridge Child Care Consultancy Service 1995: 171–2; my emphasis)

While the focus in this recommendation on *'creative discussions'* is entirely appropriate, as in this family there were older children, it is interesting that the recommendations do not also highlight the need to understand children's experience by observing and spending time with them. When he died, Paul

> had lain in urine soaked bedding and clothes for a considerable number of days. Photographs taken after his death show burns over most of his body derived from the urine staining, plus septicaemia with septic lesions at the ends of his fingers and toes. In addition he was suffering from severe pneumonia.
>
> (Bridge Child Care Consultancy Service 1995: 7)

In the month before his death there had been an anonymous allegation of abuse in relation to the eldest girl. Three weeks earlier, his mother had cancelled Paul's appointment for a vaccination because he was unwell and she had said she found it difficult to get to the clinic. She had also visited social services the week before to request financial help. Sadly no one visited the house to see what impact these difficulties were having on any of the children, or to check on Paul.

2000: Victoria Climbié died, aged eight years

Victoria was born in the Ivory Coast, where she enjoyed a healthy and happy early childhood and was described as intelligent and articulate. She was brought first to France and then to England by her aunt in April 1999, ostensibly to receive a good education. Soon after her arrival in England her aunt had contact with the local housing department and social services to seek accommodation and subsistence payments. One social worker who saw her at this time, *'recalled that Victoria seemed rather small for her age and described her as "stunted in growth", though he made no record of this in his notes'* (Laming 2003: 49).

The contrast between the well-dressed and smart appearance of the aunt and the scruffy appearance of Victoria was also noted. Another social worker who saw Victoria in May 1999 commented that she thought 'Victoria looked like an advertisement for Action Aid' and in June 1999 Victoria's posture was described by the duty social worker as, 'submissive, very quiet and timid'. However, the focus of attention was on housing and subsistence, so the meaning of these telling observations was not explored.

In July 1999 Victoria's childminder was so concerned about the numerous injuries to Victoria, that she took her to hospital. Police protection was initially provided, but she was discharged the next morning to the care of her aunt. Ten days later her aunt took her to hospital as she had suffered serious scalding to her head, necessitating an admission for 13 nights. Staff on the ward also noted numerous other marks on Victoria that included belt marks, bites and burns. However, the explanation given by the aunt for all the injuries was accepted and Victoria was again able to return home with her aunt, despite entries on the ward critical incident log describing the alarming changes in Victoria's behaviour when her aunt and Manning, her partner, visited: 'Victoria changed from being lively and vivacious to withdrawn and timid'. The relationship was described as being like that of 'master and servant'. On one occasion she wet herself while standing to attention in front of her seated aunt, who was apparently telling her off (Laming 2003: 30).

The allocated social worker spoke to Victoria briefly before her discharge, but did not notice anything untoward.

> Victoria presented as shy and withdrawn and she was reluctant to answer any of the questions that we were asking her. PC Jones then said a few words to Victoria in French and this seemed to relax and make her more comfortable.

In her note of the visit she also commented that Victoria had 'a very big smile' (Laming 2003: 153).

Victoria's first language was French, but an interpreter was not used, nor does it appear that thought was given to the significance of the observations on the ward. A less troubling impression of Victoria as 'a little ray of sunshine' was provided by a French-speaking nurse who befriended Victoria while on the ward.

When the social worker visited the home in August the focus of her attention was the need to address the accommodation problems that her aunt was requesting help with. She

> did not speak to Victoria during the course of this visit, (but) she formed the impression that Victoria was happy and seemed like the 'little ray of sunshine' described by the nurses.
>
> (Laming 2003: 31)

This reassuring view appears to have prevailed, as on the second pre-announced home visit:

> Victoria seems to have been all but ignored ... as she sat on the floor playing with a doll. The fact that she was not attending school was raised during the conversation,

> *but no questions seem to have been asked about how Victoria was spending her days.*
>
> (Laming 2003: 33)

The report concluded that:

> *The dreadful reality was that these services knew little or nothing more about Victoria at the end of the process than they did when she was first referred to Ealing Social Services.*
>
> (Laming 2003: 3)

Laming went on to emphasise the importance of accurately recording observations, as there were many disparate pieces of information known to different professionals, but not all of these were recorded or shared effectively with other professionals. An ability to articulate and bring together the concerns was missing. The inquiry found that:

> *Victoria's case, like several others which have prompted Inquiries of this nature, is one that is characterised by a consistent failure to do basic things properly.*
>
> (Laming 2003: 197)

While this may appear with hindsight to be the case, in reality it was a very complex situation, with different social services departments and hospitals involved, which further complicated the picture. This brief synopsis only touches on a few of the many issues raised in the inquiry, but what seems to emerge is that professionals clung to shreds of information that enabled them to believe that Victoria was all right; that the case was an issue of an unsettled child in a family with poverty and housing problems. This pattern of prematurely forming and clinging to a particular view, resulting in difficulty in really seeing the experience of the child, is a consistent theme that was first noted by Munro (1999) and is also noted in the biennial analysis of Serious Case Reviews (Brandon et al 2012).

2007: Peter Connolly died, aged 17 months

Peter and his family were well known to a range of statutory agencies. In December 2006, as a result of injuries that he had sustained, his name was placed on the child protection register, under the categories of physical abuse and neglect.

The overview report (Haringey Local Children Safeguarding Board 2009) found numerous occasions when Peter was seen and reported to be well, smiling and happy, as well as having a good attachment to his mother. The prevailing view of professionals was that this was a low-risk family support case, rather than one where child protection concerns were at the forefront of their minds.

In the last two months of his life Peter was seen on a number of occasions by health and social services, and the review found that:

> *During this period, and during every other period that has been reviewed, observations are made of the children, their interaction with each other and with their mother, which are reassuring to the professionals involved with the family.*

> There can be little doubt that these observations are accurate and believed to be genuine. They help to reduce the concern created when child A is injured periodically and they undermine resolve when professionals are prepared to act authoritatively.
>
> (Haringey Local Children Safeguarding Board 2009: 23)

However, it is not clear on what basis the review concluded that the observations were 'accurate', or whether they were sufficient and detailed. For example, Peter's many observed bruises were explained as being attributed by his mother to his excessively boisterous behaviour. Where observations do take place, the interpretation of what is seen when it is problematic may often be based on adult explanations.

Peter was examined by a paediatrician two days before his death. While the examining doctor was aware that he was the subject of a child protection plan, she understood that her role was to establish if there was an organic cause for his injuries and concerning behaviours, including hyperactivity and head-butting, as described by his mother. The extent of her knowledge about the previous concerns and diagnosis of abuse was thought to be limited. Unfortunately the examination was not completed, as Peter was deemed to be too unwell and miserable, possibly as a result of a virus. Numerous bruises were noted but 'not drawn on a body map'. Tragically, he died two days later and was then found to have fractured ribs and a broken back.

It is possible that a *view* about the purpose of the examination restricted the gaze of the doctor, who was then unable to see what was a highly likely reason for the injuries. Or as with the other professional contacts, perhaps there was an unconscious desire to find an explanation that avoided the disturbing possibility of serious abuse.

2012: Daniel Pelka died, aged five years

Daniel Pelka died as a result of a head injury inflicted by his mother's partner. While the Serious Case Review (Coventry Local Safeguarding Children Board 2013) concluded that this could not reasonably have been foreseen, there were many occasions when professionals had contact with Daniel, where observation might have aroused greater curiosity about his experience within the family home. The school had been concerned that Daniel was eating voraciously whenever he could. This was accompanied by concerns that in the last few months before his death he 'looked like a bag of bones', despite looking 'normal' when he had started school in the autumn. Additionally there was a long history of domestic violence between his mother and her respective partners, often involving alcohol misuse. A teaching assistant had noticed that 'his mother always seemed cross with him and that he always walked home twenty paces behind his mother' (Coventry Local Safeguarding Children Board 2013: 55).

Given that Daniel was in his first term at school and was just four and a quarter years old, these observations are highly significant, but our confidence in recognising the significance of such observations is invariably outweighed by our tendency to favour any verbal messages that we receive from adults. In this context, Daniel and his sister were unable, or too frightened, to talk about their experiences and there was a very plausible mother providing alternative explanations to address any concerns raised. As with other children referred to in this chapter:

> *Daniel appeared to have been 'invisible' as a needy child against the backdrop of his mother's controlling behaviour. His poor language skills and isolated situation meant that there was often a lack of a child focus to interventions by professionals.*
> (Coventry Local Safeguarding Children Board 2013: 6)

Given the findings of the review, it seems curious that there is no discussion of the lack of significance accorded to the observations and the value that might have been gained from a systematic approach to observing Daniel and his family.

COMMENT

As I read these and many other reviews I was struck by the reliance on how parents presented and on what they told practitioners, in contrast to the limited attention paid to listening to children, observing and understanding their lived experience. The impact of scepticism about the competence of children is illustrated in an analysis of some 45 child-abuse inquiry reports between 1973 and 1994 undertaken by Munro (1999: 752). She found that in the ten cases where communication with children was considered, what children said was listened to when it corresponded with the social worker's existing view and ignored when it did not. Hence, in three cases where the children said they were abused and it was true, they were not believed. This does suggest that careful thought needs to be given to perceptions of children and the value, or lack of value, that we accord to what they say, what they do and to time spent being with them.

What also emerges is that the reasons why the parents and carers of these children have killed them are inevitably complex, and while a better understanding of the impact of our perceptions of children should be very helpful, it is clearly not the only reason for the persistence of the difficulties in really seeing and hearing children. It does, however, provide the context that frames individual practitioners' thinking. Next, we will begin to consider issues that emerge at a personal level that may also contribute to these difficulties.

Difficulties in facing the reality of what is seen

It might initially seem, as suggested above by Laming, that '*good practice is about doing the simple things properly*' (Laming 2003: 105) and that spending time with children, observing them and ascertaining their wishes and feelings is a simple, straightforward thing to do. However, what is demonstrated by looking at child-abuse reviews for the last 40 years is that while many improvements in practice have been made, there is an extraordinarily persistent difficulty in seeing, listening to and understanding the experience of children, which may sometimes be far beyond our ability to imagine or believe.

The Serious Case Reviews into the deaths of Victoria Climbié and Daniel Pelka highlighted the difficulties in believing the evidence we are seeing, thinking about things as they are and understanding the meaning of the evidence in front of us. If we cannot believe that a parent may be harming or starving their child, we may be unable to see that it is actually happening. We readily grasp at shreds of evidence, a smile from the child or an apparently plausible explanation for an injury or bruising, to defend us from thinking about other disturbing aspects of information that contradict this, but which we cannot bear to imagine.

Rustin, drawing on psychoanalytic theory and the work of Bion (1962), suggests that *'the systematic disconnection between things which logically belong together'* is a defence mechanism, protecting us from *'the intense feelings stirred up by exposure to human cruelty'* (Rustin 2005: 12). This suggests that, in order to survive the emotionally intense and sometimes overwhelming nature of working with children and families, professionals use unconscious mechanisms to reduce their uncertainty and anxiety. One way of doing this is by disconnecting ourselves from the meaning of children's experience. Cooper and Lousada (2005: 158) suggest that *'attention to … detailed emotional observation'* was a missing dimension in the work with Victoria and her carers. Similarly Brandon et al (2012) found in their most recent biennial review of a large number of Serious Case Reviews that:

> [T]here was a sense of disconnection from the children themselves: not paying attention to children's emotional development and not thinking about what it's like to be a child living in that family or beyond the school setting; seeing the disability not the child; and most powerfully holding back from knowing the child as a person.
>
> (Brandon et al 2012: 7)

The resulting absence of meaningful engagement with and understanding of the children's experience prevents any emotional connection and so enables practitioners to reduce their anxiety and remain hopeful.

Fear

The anxiety referred to above may be further compounded by fear. The experience of visiting unwelcoming neighbourhoods and homes where there may be intimidating people, dogs, rats, smells and the fear of infection is familiar to many practitioners. Inevitably this has an impact on practice. Looking back particularly at the deaths of Paul, Victoria and Peter, practitioners working with the families expressed serious concerns about home conditions, smells, dirt and/or fear that they might be exposed to something contagious. Ferguson (2011: 95–6) discusses these fears in relation to the avoidance of touch, but it is also important to consider how they may contribute to a reluctance to spending time with a child and to visiting their home. These factors are hardly conducive to effective practice, but their impact receives scant attention within the Serious Case Reviews.

The contribution of the organisational context, in either supporting or undermining practitioners faced by such difficulties, also needs to be recognised. The absence of a containing space, enabling practitioners to reflect on and understand the difficulties they are witnessing, may result in an unconscious loss of vision, seeing but not seeing.

Conclusion

In order to understand the persistence of difficulties in seeing and hearing children this chapter has drawn on theories about the social construction and meaning of childhood and children, to explore the possible impact that these unconscious understandings may have on practitioners working with children and their families. While the view of children as vulnerable victims in need of protection may be appropriate, it may also contribute to a way of thinking where children's strengths and competence are not fully recognised. These difficulties are compounded by another prevalent perception, that children and young people are incomplete, whereas by contrast adults are complete. Neither of these perceptions is conducive to spending time with children, listening to them and thinking about the detail of their lives as children. In fact they imply that what children do and say is of less significance than what adults do; childhood is merely a preparation for the future state of being human. Such perceptions may then hinder the ability to recognise children's agency and their ability to act to shape their lives and may therefore limit recognition of what we can learn from them. Instead, reliance is placed on the views of adults, who have the power to define the issues and identify the solutions.

Within the summaries from Serious Case Reviews referred to above there is evidence of very real care and concern by the professionals who were working with the families. The reviews rightly offer a view of the children as vulnerable and in need of protection. However, one of the themes that emerges is that, despite the concerns, little time was spent being with or listening to the children, who were mostly seen very briefly and in the presence of their parents.

Another theme, highlighted by insights from psychoanalytic thinking, is that of unconscious defence mechanisms operating to protect overwhelmed professionals from seeing and attributing meaning to what they are seeing. Children become peripheral, lost in the chaos of troubled families and overwhelmed professionals. Many pieces of the jigsaw may be present, but they are all jumbled up and not connected, so enabling a reassuring piece of information to be grasped and other information to be discarded. However, as we will see, holding on to the muddle and staying with uncertainty is in fact central to effective practice. High levels of self-awareness combined with support are thus needed to enable practitioners to be aware of the operation of these difficult processes. Chapter 3 will consider some ways of becoming more aware of the way in which our own views and defence mechanisms may constrain what can be seen.

Taking it further

Brandon, M, Sidebotham, P, Bailey, S, Belderson, P, Hawley, C, Ellis, C and Megson, M (2012) *New Learning from Serious Case Reviews: A Two Year Report for 2009–2011,* Research Report DFE-RR226. London: Department for Education, www.gov.uk/government/uploads/system/uploads/attachment_data/file/184053/DFE-RR226_Report.pdf.

Ferguson, H (2011) *Child Protection Practice.* Basingstoke: Palgrave Macmillan.

James, A and James, A (2008) *Key Concepts in Childhood Studies.* London: Sage.

Jenks, C (2005) *Childhood*, 2nd edn. Abingdon: Routledge.

Laming, Lord (2003) *The Victoria Climbié Inquiry*, CM 5730. London: The Stationery Office, www.gov.uk/government/uploads/system/uploads/attachment_data/file/273183/5730.pdf.

Munro, E (2011) *Munro Review of Child Protection: Interim Report: The Child's Journey*, DFE-00010-2011. London: Department for Education, www.gov.uk/government/collections/munro-review.

References

Alderson, P (2000) *Young Children's Rights: Exploring Beliefs, Principles and Practice*. London: JKP.

Arnold, E (1987) *Whose Child? The Report of the Public Inquiry into the Death of Tyra Henry*. London Borough of Lambeth.

Bion, W (1962) *Learning from Experience*. London: Heinemann.

Brandon, M, Sidebotham, P, Bailey, S, Belderson, P, Hawley, C, Ellis, C and Megson, M (2012) *New Learning from Serious Case Reviews: A Two Year Report for 2009–2011,* Research Report DFE-RR226. London: Department for Education, www.gov.uk/government/uploads/system/uploads/attach-ment_data/file/184053/DFE-RR226_Report.pdf (accessed 22 September 2015).

Blom-Cooper, L et al (1985) *A Child in Trust: The Report of the Panel of Enquiry into the Circumstances Surrounding the Death of Jasmine Beckford*. London Borough of Brent.

The Bridge Child Care Consultancy Service (1995) *Paul: Death through Neglect*. London: Islington ACPC/The Bridge.

Children Act (1989). London: Her Majesty's Stationery Office.

Coventry Local Safeguarding Children Board (2013) *Daniel Pelka Serious Case Review: Final Overview Report*. Coventry Local Safeguarding Children Board.

Cooper, A and Lousada J (2005) *Borderline Welfare: Feeling and Fear of Feeling in Modern Welfare*. London, Karnac.

Cunningham, H (2006) *The Invention of Childhood*. London: BBC Books.

Daniel, P and Ivatts, J (1998) *Children and Social Policy*. Basingstoke: Macmillan.

DHSS (Department of Health and Social Security) (1974) *Report of the Committee of Inquiry into the Care and Supervision Provided in Relation to Maria Colwell*. London: HMSO.

Featherstone, B, White, S and Monis, K (2014) *Reimagining Child Protection*. Bristol, Policy Press.

Ferguson, H (2011) *Child Protection Practice*. Basingstoke: Palgrave Macmillan.

Haringey Local Children Safeguarding Board (2009) *Serious Case Review, Executive Summary*. Haringey Local Safeguarding Children Board, www.haringeylscb.org/sites/haringeylscb/files/executive_summary_peter_final.pdf (accessed 22 September 2015).

Hendrick, H (2005) *Child Welfare and Social Policy: An Essential Reader*. Bristol, Policy Press.

James, A, Jenks, C and Prout, A (1998) *Theorizing Childhood*. Cambridge, Polity Press.

Laming, Lord (2003) *The Victoria Climbié Inquiry*, CM 5730. London: The Stationery Office, www.gov.uk/government/uploads/system/uploads/attachment_data/file/273183/5730.pdf (accessed 22 September 2015).

Lansdown, G (1995) *Taking Part: Children's Participation in Decision Making*. London, Public Policy Research.

Mayall, B (1996) *Children, Health and the Social Order*. Buckingham, Open University Press.

(2002) *Towards a Sociology for Childhood*. Buckingham, Open University Press.

Munro, E (1999) Common Errors of Reasoning in Child Protection Work. *Child Abuse and Neglect*, 23(8): 745–58.

Munro, E (2011) *Munro Review of Child Protection: Interim Report: The Child's Journey*, DFE-00010-2011. London: Department for Education, www.gov.uk/government/collections/munro-review (accessed 22 September 2015).

Munro, E, Brown, R, Sempik, J and Ward, H, with Owen, C (2011) *Scoping Review to Draw Together Data on Child Injury and Safeguarding and to Compare the Position of England with That in Other Countries*, Research Report DFE-RR083. London: Department for Education, www.gov.uk/government/uploads/system/uploads/attachment_data/file/182284/DFE-RR083.pdf (accessed 7 July 2015).

Pritchard, C and Williams, R (2010) Comparing Possible 'Child-Abuse-Related Deaths' in England and Wales with the Major Developed Countries 1974–2006: Signs of Progress? *British Journal of Social Work*, 40: 1700–18, www.nspcc.org.uk/preventing-abuse/child-protection-system/legal-definition-child-rights-law/legal-definitions/ (accessed 19 July 2015).

Qvortrup, J (1994) Childhood Matters: An Introduction, in Qvortrup, J, Bardy, M, Sgritta, G and Wintersberger, H (eds) *Childhood Matters: Social Theory, Practice and Politics*. Aldershot: Avebury Press.

Rustin, M E (2005) Conceptual Analysis of Critical Moments in Victoria Climié's Life. *Child and Family Social Work*, 10: 11–20.

2 Approaches to observation

PIA PARRY

This chapter will introduce:

- the development of observational studies;
- a range of approaches to observation;
- behavioural and experiential observations;
- advantages and disadvantages of different approaches.

People in different occupations and different professions can mean very different things when they use the word 'observation'. This chapter will introduce the reader to a range of methods of observation, explaining how and why these methods were developed and the different purposes that they may be used for. Examples of the ways in which the various observation methods can be used in practice are given later in the chapter.

Methods of observation

Methods of observation can be broadly grouped into two different approaches. The first approach entails recording and monitoring the behaviour of children, referred to here as behavioural approaches. The second approach is experiential and records behaviours, feelings and relationships; it is informed by psychoanalytic and psychodynamic thinking. It can be described as naturalistic, experiential and holistic.

Observation can be used for *research*-based ethnographic enquiry to:

- explore the world around us and the people and cultures within it;
- collect rich data for analysis;
- develop and broaden our understanding of humanity;
- see at first hand what is happening;
- witness verbal and non-verbal interactions between the child and others.

As a method of research, *child-watching* (Cotton et al 2010) allows the researcher to observe and understand the child's experiences in order to provide appropriate support. It can generate both qualitative and quantitative data in different settings such as school, nursery, community or faith-based group or in the child's own family setting.

Observation can help us to *understand individuals and groups*, their lived experiences and their interactions with others. It can therefore form a vital part of an assessment of a child and their family, as it provides empirical evidence of what is actually happening. Information from the observations can then be used as the basis for decision-making and planning interventions to address any needs that have been identified.

Child observation is used as a tool for the *training and development* of psychoanalysts, social workers, early years workers, teachers and health professionals. Depending on the method used and the age of the child observed, it may enhance the student's understanding of themselves, their cultural biases and their knowledge and understanding of child development and play. For professionals working with children and families these are critical areas of professional and personal development, as without such understanding any judgement made is inevitably skewed, albeit unconsciously, by personal experience.

The development of different approaches to observation

Child observation has developed in response to changing views about childhood and the development of knowledge and understanding in relation to researching young children's lives.

Observation studies are generally considered to have evolved from the work of Charles Darwin, the naturalist and geologist famous for his theory of evolution, explaining how species have evolved over time. One of his observational studies (1877) focused on a biography of his son as a baby and his expression of emotions, which he published 37 years later.

Observations gave many of the key theorists evidence for their hypotheses. Sigmund Freud, the Austrian neurologist who founded psychoanalysis, included case studies as a series of observations in his seminal work *Psychopathology of Everyday Life* (1914). He studied unconscious processes such as dreams and neuroses while using talking therapies to help his patients recover from trauma and distress. His work on psychoanalytic observations and psychoanalysis are reported in his earlier work entitled *Three Essays on the Theory of Sexuality* (1905).

Psychoanalytic observations have been carried out by researchers and practitioners working in the fields of both education and psychoanalysis. Susan Isaacs, a pioneering educational psychologist and psychoanalyst, based her theories on the close observation of young children. Her observations, described as naturalistic, took place as children played at the Malting House School, where she created the notion that play is children's work. She noted that observations could help us to understand the child's wishes and their thoughts by entering the magical world of childhood, without interfering in it (Isaacs 1952).

Theorist	Method of observation	Findings	Relevance
Darwin (1877)	Observations of his son written as a diary	Described conscious and unconscious communications in his young child	Study of very young babies given relevance
Freud, English translation (1914) and Klein (1935)	Clinical observations	Psychoanalytic development	Unconscious processes caused by early childhood trauma may become manifest in later behaviour
Bick (1964)	Infant observations	Insight into baby and maternal anxieties	Preparation for psychoanalytic work
Isaacs (1952)	Observation in a nursery school	Understanding of social and intellectual growth	Learning from observations to assess children's progress
Piaget (1952)	Observations of his own child	Cognitive development in stages	Significance of child development knowledge to observations
Bion (1962)	Child observation	Development of the mind	Understanding containment of feelings
Fraiberg (1975)	Therapeutic use of child observation	Intergenerational emotional links	Detailing need for parental observations

Figure 2.1 Selected theoretical developments

In 1948 Esther Bick, a psychoanalyst, introduced infant observation as part of the training of child psychotherapists at the Tavistock Clinic in London. While Bick continued to use the naturalistic approach favoured by ethnologists, she used psychoanalytic thinking to inform the reflection and analysis of the observational experience.

The Tavistock method of observation as originally practised by Bick required students to be supported to observe a baby through two years of early infancy and to become attuned to the child and his or her growing relationships. Observations were carried out in weekly visits for one hour, at the same time each week, in the child's home. Students were required to maintain a receptive stance, rather than passive or active. They were advised not to record during the observation as this would create a barrier and limit receptivity, but to write up the observation afterwards as a free-flowing narrative. Students were then supported in their reflections and growing understanding of unconscious communications by a seminar group led by a trained facilitator. This process gave students insights into their own thoughts, feelings and assumptions, as well as allowing them to learn about the experiences, both conscious and unconscious, of the child they observed and their parents or carers.

Filmed recordings of child observations began with James Robertson and his wife in 1952 (Robertson and Robertson 1952). Working closely with John Bowlby, the Robertsons are known for their empirical filmed observations of young children throughout the 1950s and 1960s (www.robertsonfilms.info). They used psychoanalytic frameworks to highlight the emotional experiences of the children they filmed during periods of painful separation from their main carers. Their films revealed both conscious and unconscious processes in the children and their carers and these films have, subsequently, had a very significant impact on the provision of care for young children when separated from their parents. They continue to make uncomfortable viewing, providing graphic demonstrations of young children's responses to separation and loss.

During the 1970s the Tavistock psychoanalytic model of early infant observation was introduced to a wider range of professionals and broadened to include observation of young children. It is from this tradition and the guidance produced by the Central Council for Training in Social Work (CCETSW 1991) that current practice has developed in some social work and early childhood training.

Rustin (2009) reviewed the model 60 years after it began being used in the training of psychotherapists in London. Rustin found that the model developed by Bick had been disseminated to international audiences across the world and 'continues to inspire' (2009: 40) professionals and students. The model has developed through research and combined learning from the people who have used it with their findings published through the International Journal of Infant Observation and Its Applications (1997-).

COMMENT

Different methods of observation provide different types of qualitative and quantitative information and each has advantages and disadvantages that need to be carefully considered in relation to what observers hope to achieve and learn. The decision about which method of observation should be used depends upon the purpose of the observation, how much time is available, the availability of support and supervision, and the knowledge and skills of the observer.

Behavioural methods

Some methods of observation may be regarded as providing a greater degree of objectivity, providing information that may be regarded as more factual, rather than opinions which are more subjective. Behavioural methods are often associated with being more quantitative and objective.

Behavioural methods monitor and record changes in the way children develop, for example changes in their speech and language, physical movements, learning and in their mastery of skills. From observations it is possible to create charts to describe phases of development which can be linked to ages, for example Mary Sheridan's charts (1960s). Although there are criticisms about the use of charts because they offer a model of development that not all children follow due to differences of culture, class or ability (Taylor 2004), they do offer a framework for the study of child development. Despite their limitations, behavioural methods of observation have advantages when used in quantitative studies on groups or individual children. They allow for systematic collection of large amounts of data and the studies can be replicated. Generally these methods of observation create an objective record of the findings which can be used to create a theory or hypothesis.

Behavioural methods of observation can have advantages in helping practitioners understand the range of behaviours any child may present and recognise where a child's development may be different. The recognition of these differences in behaviours should lead us to ask questions about what might be going on for the child. Observations can help to capture a detailed picture of what the child does, with whom, and can highlight their ability and their interests. This information can be used to assess and plan the next steps in extending the child's learning or play, so this method is particularly helpful in schools. Behavioural methods of observation are used in educational settings, with the records forming part of the child's list of achievements. The record may include photographs, videos, written reports, charts and examples of work with comments about routine and spontaneous events. Parents and children have access to these records, which are updated daily and summarised by the child's key worker.[1]

Any difficulties children may be experiencing can be identified as early as possible and a plan developed to respond to the holistic needs of the child. This may involve observations of a more focused nature being carried out over a period of time but avoids emphasising the difficulty by considering the wider needs of the child.

Behavioural methods provide mostly quantitative data about the child and can answer questions such as:

*   How often does this behaviour occur?

*   Can this child do (an activity such as writing)?

*   What happens when (an event happens)?

*   Who interacts with the child or vice versa?

*   What are the preferred or rejected choices the child makes?

This group of methods includes sampling, checklists, rating scales and 'target child'. They can be helpful in recording patterns of behaviours, activities which the child participates in and their ability in a defined set of tasks.

---

[1] Key worker – a person allocated to the child and family who will build a trusting relationship and take responsibility for coordination and sharing of information.

Activity

As you read the next section, think about a child you know or have worked with and consider the sort of questions you might be able to ask using one of the behavioural methods below.

What would you learn?

Time sampling

Time sampling can be used to determine the frequency of a child's behaviour within a given time frame, or to observe the child within a given timeframe. It requires a prepared proforma with agreement on the focus and purpose of the observation.

The following example of time sampling was introduced to help staff gain a more accurate picture of this child, Dara James, aged three years.

Name of the child: Dara James	Date: 3rd February 2014
Name of the observer: Brian Thompson	Place of observation: Nursery school
Brief description of the purpose: Dara plays mainly in the garden each day and the observer wants to monitor how much time Dara spends outside in the sand play. This time sampling observation will record Dara's activities for ten minutes each hour to see how often she is playing in the sand	
Consent obtained from: Dara's mother	

Start time	Duration	Observations	Further notes
9:15	Ten minutes	Dara arrived at 9:12 am and went directly to the outside sand play area	Dara in the garden near the sand play area but not playing with the sand
10:15	Ten minutes	Dara seemed reluctant to sit indoors at the table for snack time	Snack time
11:15	Ten minutes	Dara appears to be wandering around not settling to any one activity	Dara wanted to go in the garden but it was raining heavily, so she stood by the window
12:15	Ten minutes	Dara outside playing on the swing	Three boys playing in the sand

Figure 2.2 *Example of time sampling*

The time-sampling charts allow data to be collected and evaluated which may help with planning for the child. In the example shown in Figure 2.2 the child has spent only a brief amount of time playing in the sand and seems reluctant to return to the sand when a group of three boys are playing there. Dara may have a schema of play which does not include other children or she may prefer solitary play. Further observations may elicit more detail and suggest other patterns of behaviour.

The advantages of this method are that it is accessible to the child, parents and any member of staff, it is easy to use once the proforma is developed and it can be used to observe several children at the same time. The observations can be repeated at different intervals to build up a picture of Dara's behaviour over time.

The disadvantages are that it may limit the observer's view of the child's behaviour to the agreed focus and it offers no explanation from the child or others about why the behaviours change.

Event sampling

Event sampling has similar characteristics to time sampling and focuses on a specific 'event' or behaviour. It requires a proforma or chart to record the details of the event and its possible antecedents.

In the example of event sampling shown in Figure 2.3 the staff are keen to explore Dara's behaviour around a particular event. Their observations can be undertaken over a number of days and by a number of different staff before reflecting, comparing and discussing their ideas.

The event-sampling method collects a set of data based around the 'event'. In the example (Figure 2.3), the purpose is to try and understand what triggers the behaviours observed at this time. Planning for Dara at home time can begin once there is an improved understanding of what happens around this event. The event sampling record needs to include actions and activities carried out by others as well as Dara to build a more complete picture of this event. On this occasion it seemed as if Dara was reluctant to admit she had been playing in the sand and it might be helpful for her key worker to carry out a more detailed observation of the sand play and perhaps a visit to see Dara at home so her behaviour can be reflected upon further. Discussion with Dara's mother may shed some light on this behaviour and her expectations about her daughter.

Observations of 'events' can be held at particular times of the day or around certain activities or specific behaviours. Some professions use a technique called 'applied behaviour analysis' to study human behaviour – this is often in the context of using behaviourist approaches to change behaviour. For example, rewarding certain behaviours in order to reinforce them.

Observations do not, in themselves, prescribe methods of intervention, but there are relationships between particular types of action and the method of observation employed. Sampling methods of observation can generally be linked to instructional methods of intervention, such as teaching. They are often employed by educationalists and some health professionals, such as health visitors.

Name of the child:	Date:
Dara James	12th February 2014
Name of the observer:	**Place of observation:**
Brian Thompson	Nursery school

Brief description of the purpose:

Dara appears to play on her own in the sand each day. This event sampling observation will record Dara's activities

Consent obtained from:

Dara's mother

Time and length of observation	Activity	Observations and notes
3:30 pm for 15 minutes	Sand play	Dara is sitting, playing in the sand, running fingers through dry sand, laughing and dribbling sand through her fingers in front of her face. One of the other children (DZ) was called in to go home with his mother and Dara stood up and brushed the sand off her clothes and hurried inside as if she had been involved in something she should not have done. When her mother arrived Dara was keen to show her a painting she had made earlier. Her mother asked what else she had been doing and Dara said she had been 'reading'.

Figure 2.3 *Example of event sampling*

Checklists

Checklists and tests are used by a wide variety of professionals from the time a child is born through the whole life span. They can be helpful in determining what tasks or activities can be achieved by an individual and what they may need further help or practice with. Checklists include developmental charts (Sheridan, Sharma and Cockerill 2007), educational profiles, Portage planning (Portage is a home-visiting educational service for pre-school children with additional support needs and their families), assessment and action records for looked-after children and some assessment forms used in wider social work practice. The advantages of using checklists in observation can be their simplicity and universality. In multi-agency work with professionals from different disciplines it can be helpful to create a shared checklist with agreed definitions so assessments can be shared.

Rating scales

Rating scales can be added to checklists as a way of grading responses. The most common rating scale is the 'five point' example. For instance, in the checklist shown in Figure 2.4 the staff are monitoring Dara's mother's responses.

In the sample checklist (Figure 2.4) a rating scale has been added to give greater detail to the observations.

Name of the child:	Date:
Dara James	17th February 2014
Name of the observer:	**Place of observation:**
Brian Thompson	Nursery school
Purpose of rating scale observation:	
To monitor what Dara says about her own behaviour and her mother's responses	
Consent obtained from:	
Dara's mother, who has expressed concerns over Dara's progress at nursery	

Observation	Not at all	Sometimes	Fairly often	Often	Non-stop
Dara playing with another child					
Dara using sentences to talk with another child					
Dara having physical contact with others					

Figure 2.4 *Example of rating scales*

Activity

What are the benefits of using this approach?

What is missing in these observations?

The simplicity and clear focus of this approach means that evidence can easily be gathered in relation to specific, previously agreed issues. One of the disadvantages of using this type of record may be the limitations in terms of quality. For example, the checklist

(Figure 2.4) asks the observer to note when Dara is communicating with others but the observer could also acknowledge Dara's increasing vocabulary or her preference for certain people or toys. Further, there is no record here of Dara's emotional state or well-being. These could be gained from using an experiential approach underpinned by reflection and analysis.

The 'target child' method

The 'target child' method of observation (Sylva, Roy and Painter 1980) gives the observer the opportunity to focus on all aspects of the behaviour of a child for a short period of time (approximately 20 minutes) in order that a record can be made of the child's educational, learning and social activities, as well as the interactions with the adult in the educational setting. This method is used mainly by teaching and support staff in schools, and its main advantage is that it focuses the observations through use of a grid which observers can complete and share with parents and colleagues.

Observations of Dara as a 'target child' show her to have physical, cognitive and social skills which she uses in play. Earlier observations and concerns from her mother suggested that Dara may have difficulties in some aspects of her development, but the more holistic observation used in Figure 2.5 shows Dara to be a confident girl with developing skills.

Journals and diaries

Journals and diaries could be categorised as behavioural and/or experiential, depending on the approach taken. They can provide running records of observations, focusing particularly on actions, or they may incorporate feelings and be more holistic. With technological advances there has been an increase in blogs, video footage and photographs to record and enhance observations.

Some children can participate and co-construct their records to provide an enduring account of their experiences. Kanyal (2014) discusses the advantages of presenting the records from the child's perspective (first person) while acknowledging the record will not truly convey the full thoughts of the child, but rather what the child selects to record.

> ### *Activity*
>
> *Make a list of all the methods referred to above.*
>
> *Write down next to each one the circumstances in which this approach might be useful.*
>
> *What are the advantages and disadvantages of using this method in your workplace?*

Name of the child:	Date:
Dara James	27th February 2014
Name of the observer:	**Place of observation:**
Brian Thompson	Nursery school

Brief description of the purpose:

Observation of Dara with another child (MH) in the book corner

Consent obtained from:

Dara's mother

Time	Observations	Further notes
9:15	Dara arrived at 9:12 am and went directly to the outside play area where a book corner had been created under a large sun umbrella. Dara and MH settled into one of the bean bags together and looked as if they were reading *The Very Hungry Caterpillar.*	
	Dara appeared to read aloud the number parts and MH giggled; '*he ate one apple ... two pears ... three plums ... four strawberries ... five oranges ...*' Dara used her fingers to show MH how many the caterpillar ate. The story seemed to be retold from memory and recognition of the images rather than from the words. When the story ended Dara said '*let's go and make some caterpillars then we can eat them*'. They ran off to find dough and made worms then rolled them in the sand and pretended to eat them – laughing loudly.	

Figure 2.5 *Example of target child observation*

Holistic experiential observation

The next section of this chapter extends the notion of holistic approaches in child observation, where the experience of the observer is included in the reflection and analysis. Experiential observations are often linked to qualitative approaches which are more subjective and linked to the experiences of participants, both observers and those being observed

Fawcett (1996: 3) compared the experience of being an observer to walking through the park listening to birds singing. She suggested that being able to hear the birds was one thing, being able to detect which sort of bird was singing was another, and understanding 'why' they are singing would be the final part of the experience. This, she argued, could be compared to having a detailed picture of a child being observed, understanding both the context and the experience for the child.

In order to be fully attuned, we also need to have some understanding of ourselves and, most importantly, the 'lens' through which we see others. This 'lens' describes the way we each see and understand the world; it is made up of our conscious and unconscious experiences, our values, beliefs, memories and expectations. The 'lens' is the filter of our assumptions about others and how we think they *should* behave based on our own experience and individual view. When we observe others we *expect* to see them behave in certain ways and we *measure* their experience by our own. For example, observing a young baby crying may be experienced by the observer as a reaction to their presence in the room, the assumption being that the baby's behaviour may be linked to them. There could be all sorts of other reasons for the baby to cry, and careful reflection and analysis may help the observer to understand this behaviour, just like understanding why the birds are singing. It is important to note that sometimes this 'understanding' of others can be elusive and we are left *not knowing* (Bion 1962) why a certain behaviour or feeling has been experienced. As we saw in the previous chapter, this state of *not knowing* and uncertainty is an important part of the process of understanding children's experience.

The image of walking through the park being oblivious to the sights and sounds around us could reasonably be compared to the experience of a busy, preoccupied social worker, where the task becomes the focus instead of the child and their thoughts and feelings. There has been an increasing tension between social work as a 'technical, rational' task and social work as relationship-based practice where children's thoughts and feelings matter. Observational studies can help to bridge the gap between the competing demands of task and process so that we make the best use of the time we have with children in their day-to-day lives.

Unlike behavioural approaches to observation, this holistic approach is explicitly experiential. Observers are encouraged to be emotionally present and to reflect on the meaning of the experience for them, as well as for the child. The process of reflection is most readily accomplished with the support of experienced colleagues who can discuss the feelings evoked by the observation (Rustin 2009). The ability to practice effective reflection needs to be supported by a clear process, which will be discussed in the next chapter and will develop with practice and self-awareness.

Parton (2012) criticises the trend towards practice which *deflects* professionals from working face to face with children and which increases the tendency towards bureaucracy. He argues that there is a growing need to support professionals working with children and families so they can feel confident in using their skills to build relationships and appreciate the child's experience. The trend towards avoidance of emotional relationships was highlighted by a government report (DCSF 2009) which suggested that social workers, on average, spent less than 10 per cent of their time having direct contact with children and 15 per cent (Burke 2012) with their service users overall. Although pressures from other administrative tasks are blamed for the lack of contact with children, there may be other reasons associated with emotions such as fear, which deter professionals from greater involvement, which will be discussed further in the next chapter.

Observations can offer the opportunity to reverse this trend of deflection by validating time spent with children in the context of their family or day-to-day living situation. In order to help develop a more detailed understanding of the child's lived experience professionals need time to build relationships with them. Ultimately, more detailed and reflective observations can lead to improved decision-making when considering the needs of each child or young person.

The relationship a child has with others needs to be observed and understood so that informed decisions about the child's circumstances can be made; how the child feels about each member of their family and network will depend on any number of individual factors. Relationships will vary over time and alter as a result of changes in the child's life. Trying to fully understand and appreciate other people's relationships is not easy when they fall outside our own 'frame of reference' or experience. Observers therefore need to be aware of their own limitations, prejudices and emotional states. It takes time and reflection to build a relationship and develop attunement to others' experiences.

Non-participant observation

Non-participant observation is a contested notion (Keiding 2010). All the methods of observation described above inevitably involve participation by the observer, no matter how much they wish to remain invisible, neutral and objective. Just 'being there' has an impact on the situation, and knowing this leads us to question our own thoughts, feelings and values. Although the impact of the observer's presence can be minimised by careful preparation, observers need to consider the impact of their presence at every stage.

Activity

Reflect on your experiences of being with different people – an older member of your family, a new colleague at work or a young child. Do you feel different depending on who you are with? How does your behaviour change?

COMMENT

Most observations require the observer to 'stand back' but their presence is known to the child and will have an impact on the way that the child acts. The older the child, the more intrusive observations may be. Observers therefore need to recognise and reflect on the impact of their presence not only on the child, but also on the child's environment, the child's carers and the child's interactions with others.

> [R]elationships with people who care for and about children are the golden thread in children's lives, and [...] the quality of a child's relationships is the lens through which we should view what we do and plan to do.
>
> (Care Inquiry 2013: 2)

Relationships are the key to effective professional practice based on openness, honesty and integrity. We can use opportunities for observation to help us understand the lived experience of each child we have professional contact with. Observation requires continuous reflection:

knowledge of self as well as knowledge and understanding of developmental, educational and psychoanalytic theories. It requires good interpersonal skills and an understanding of different observational methods. This does not mean that observation can only be carried out by knowledgeable and skilled practitioners, but the ability to understand the child's lived experience will be enhanced by having a greater understanding of theory and insight into our own 'inner worlds' (Bion 1962) and by learning through experience. Our 'inner worlds' are made up from attachments, love, hate and ambivalence; developing a deeper understanding of our own inner world will help us to understand the meanings we apply to the behaviour and experiences of others.

The holistic, experiential approach to observation can be used to record and describe the total experience of the observed child and will thus include interactions with others as well as the emotional dimension of what is observed. Holistic experiential observations can be carried out in a structured environment such as school, nursery or other setting, or in the child's own home or any unstructured environment. They can offer insights into the *qualities of the nature of relationships, play and repeated interactions*' (Fleming 2004, p 227).

The advantages of using this approach are that it can provide detailed accounts of day-to-day life, it does not require printed forms, it can be recorded orally or in writing, it can be carried out by many different professionals and it can be used for professionals to learn from.

The observer is required to suspend judgement and remain in the moment, so that they are open to everything they are observing, as well as being conscious of their own thoughts and feelings as they observe (Trowell and Miles 1991). The observer's thoughts and feelings may have been aroused because what they are observing touches on something in their own experience (transference), but they may also have been aroused by something in the child's unconscious communication (counter-transference). These concepts will be explained in more depth in Chapter 5, but it is important to note here that they are integral to this approach to observation, which recognises that observation can never be objective: the observer is a part of what is observed. Hence, it is crucial that the observer records in a free-flowing way everything that they observe (Ellis et al 1998).

Initially observers often find that they struggle to record the detail of a child's play, thinking that perhaps it is too mundane or appears repetitive. With practice, observers quickly begin to grasp the significance of what they are seeing. We will explore ways of developing skills in holistic experiential observation in the next chapter, but it is useful first to think about what could be revealed by using this approach when observing Dara and comparing it with what we have observed when using the behavioural approaches described above.

Activity

Using this experiential method of observation, imagine the situation of Dara (Figure 2.2 above).

What thoughts and feelings might be in your observation?

Ethics in observation

Many professionals are well versed in gaining ethical approval before undertaking research but often overlook or diminish the need for seeking approval for observations. Informed consent is required for all forms of social research, including observation. Participants, whether they are adults or children, have a right to know and to participate in decisions about what will happen to the information being recorded about them. Hence, whatever approach to observation is used, there are ethical issues to consider.

It is important that those who are being observed know that they are being observed, why they are being observed and what purpose any information gained may serve. This can be challenging when student observers are 'in training', where they need to undertake some analysis and reflection on their own 'lens' as well as making comments about what they observe. It is important to find an approach that separates personal learning and reflection, while enabling parents and children to see the records pertaining to them.

Research into children's understanding and their capacity to give meaningful consent (Alderson 2000) would suggest that even very young children are able to take a view about what they want to happen to them and what they are comfortable with. In her research Alderson found that young children's comprehension is considerably greater than their ability to express themselves verbally. By the age of 20 months many children will listen to simple explanations, take adults by the hand and pull them towards where they want to go, while pushing others away who they do not want to be present. The word 'no' may be in frequent use, accompanied by very clear body language and sometimes crying when thwarted or ignored. While it is not suggested that a child of this age may be able to understand an explanation about observation, they will be able to demonstrate confusion, discomfort or pleasure in relation to an observer's presence.

The United Nations Convention on the Rights of the Child (UNCRC) (United Nations 1989) states in Article 12 that children should have the right to express their views in all matters that concern them. Good practice in observations should therefore include consideration of child-centred informed assent (Kanyal 2014) and legal (parental) consent. Practical approaches to this, with a suggested pro forma agreement, will be discussed in the next chapter. The difference between assent and consent is quite subtle, with each child needing to be asked for their assent (agreement) to being observed whist their parent or other gatekeeper needs to give consent (permission). It is also important to be aware that the Gillick ruling established that the legal right of a parent to make decisions about what is right

> yields to the child's right to make his own decisions when he reaches a sufficient understanding and intelligence to be capable of making up his own mind on the matter requiring decision.
>
> (Gillick v West Norfolk & Wisbech Area Health Authority 1985)

This means that if a child or young person is able to properly understand the request to be observed, their consent is required and the view of the parent may be disregarded.

With younger children, legal consent in the form of written permission needs to be obtained from the person or persons holding parental responsibility for the child before assent can be obtained from the child. In some situations the 'gatekeeper', usually the manager of the setting, also needs to give written permission for the observation to take place.

Practice issue

In a recent cohort of student observers, one student was told that parents in the school give 'blanket' consent to observations and it was therefore not necessary to obtain assent from the children being observed or their legal parent.

Activity

What you would do as an observer in this situation?

COMMENT

Given the clarity of the UNCRC on this matter and the Professional Capabilities Framework for social workers, it is appropriate to seek assent, even where you have been told that prior agreement has been given, demonstrating respect for the child and consideration of the child's feelings. Moreover, in accordance with the Gillick ruling, the consent of the children and young people concerned may also be required.

Conclusion

This chapter has considered various different methods of observation, drawing a distinction between behavioural and experiential approaches. The development of observation as a means of research stems from Darwin's work in 1877. Freud (1914) introduced the inner world of unconscious communication to us, where fears and fantasies directly affected behaviours. He generated theory and frameworks which are still used today, although they are applied with greater consideration of difference and diversity.

The main advantage of using observation as a method of understanding children and their families is that it can help us to understand the lived experiences of the child. There are advantages and disadvantages for each method of observation and the choice of method depends on two main issues: the purpose of the observation and the knowledge, skills and experience of the observer. Secondary issues include practicality, time and available resources.

Behavioural methods offer greater reliability, in research terms, than others. This means that the observation can be repeated and findings can lead to a hypothesis. Experiential methods of observation help us to understand the experiences of the child and generate deeper understanding of ourselves and the 'lens' through which we observe.

The experiential approach encourages deeper free-flowing thought and recording from the observer. It is a readily available method which supports self-development as well as the ability to enter the world of childhood. Observers need the emotional resources and capacity to stay open and the ability to connect with others, as well as more practical arrangements, such as having an experienced supervisor and time and support to undertake such work.

The impact of the observer requires consideration in all methods; similarly, other factors such as the health and well-being of the child need to be considered in situations where observations are used to assess the child. A child may present very differently when they are tired or unwell. Ethical issues of assent, consent, integrity and respect all form part of the planning, implementation and ending of observational studies. Recording practices will vary according to the method used and local practices employed.

Throughout this chapter there are compelling arguments for using experiential methods in child observation and suggestions for activities which will enable readers to select the right method for their observation. Practice will improve both confidence and ability in the observer to undertake observations as part of their day-to-day role.

Taking it further

Fawcett, M (2009) *Learning through Child Observation*. London: Jessica Kingsley.

Hobart, C and Frankel, J (2004) *A Practical Guide to Child Observation and Assessment*, 3rd edn. Cheltenham: Nelson Thornes.

International Journal of Infant Observation and Its Applications. London: Routledge, www.tandfonline. com/toc/riob20/current#.VeciWCVVikp.

LeRiche, P and Tanner, K (1998) *Observation and its Application to Social Work*. London: Jessica Kingsley.

References

Alderson, P (2000) *Young Children's Rights: Exploring Beliefs, Principles and Practice.* London: Jessica Kingsley.

Bick, E (1964) Notes on Infant Observation in Psychoanalytic Training. *International Journal of Psychoanalysis* 45: 558–66.

Bion, W (1962) *Learning from Experience.* London: Heinemann.

Burke, C (2012) Social Workers Putting in Longer Hours. *Guardian*, 25 September.

Care Inquiry (2013) *Making not Breaking: Building Relationships for Our Most Vulnerable Children. Findings and Recommendations of the Care Inquiry Launched in the House of Commons on 30 April 2013*, www.nuffieldfoundation.org/sites/default/files/files/Care%20Inquiry%20-%20 Full%20Report%20April%202013.pdf (accessed 22 September 2015).

Central Council for Training in Social Work (CCETSW) (1991) *Rules and Requirements for the Diploma in Social Work*. London: CCETSW.

(1991) *The Teaching of Child Care in the Diploma in Social Work*. London: CCETSW.

Cotton, D R E, Stokes, A and Cotton, P A (2010) Using Observational Methods to Research the Student Experience. *Journal of Geography in Higher Education*, 34(3): 463–73.

Darwin, C (1877) A Biographical Sketch of an Infant, first published in *Mind*, 2(7): 285–94, Darwin Online, http://darwin-online.org.uk/content/frameset?pageseq=1&itemID=F1779&viewtype=text (accessed 22 September 2015).

Department for Children, Schools and Families (DCSF) (2009) *How Social Workers Spend Their Time: An Analysis of the Key Issues that Impact on Practice Pre- and Post-Implementation of the Integrated Children's System*, Research Report DCSF-RR087. London: DCSF.

Elfer, P (2012) Psychoanalytic Methods of Observation as a Research Tool for Exploring Young Children's Nursery Experience. *International Journal of Social Research Methodology*, 15(3): 225–238.

Ellis, L, Lasson, I and Solomon, R (1998) *Keeping Children in Mind: A Model of Child Observation Practice*. Chelmsford: Central Council for Education and Training in Social Work.

Fawcett, M (1996) *Learning through Child Observation*. London: Jessica Kingsley.

Fleming, S. (2004) The Contribution of Psychoanalytical Observation in Child Protection Assessments. *Journal of Social Work Practice*, 18: 223–38.

Fraiberg, S, Adelson, E and Shapiro, V (1975) *Ghosts in the Nursery*. Available at mhfamilypsychology.com.

Freud, S (1905) *Three Essays on the Theory of Sexuality*, trans. J Strachey. Eastford, USA: Martino Fine Books.

Freud, S (1914) *Psychopathology of Everyday Life*, trans. A A Brill. New York: Macmillan.

Gillick v West Norfolk & Wisbech Area Health Authority (1985) British and Irish Legal Information Institute, UKHL 7 (17 October 1985).

Isaacs, S (1952) *The Educational Value of the Nursery School*. London: Headly Brothers Ltd.

Isaacs, S (1971) *The Nursery Years: The Mind of the Child from Birth to Six Years*. London: Routledge.

Kanyal, M (ed.) (2014) *Children's Rights 0–8: Promoting Participation in Education and Care*. Abingdon: Routledge.

Keiding, T (2010) Observing Participating Observation: A Re-description Based on Systems Theory. *Forum: Qualitative Social Research*, 11(3): Art 11.

Parton, N (2012) The Munro Review of Child Protection: An Appraisal. *Children and Society* 26(2): 150–162.

Piaget, J (1952) *The Origins of Intelligence in Children*. New York: International Universities Press.

Piaget, J (1957) *Construction of Reality in the Child*. London: Routledge.

Robertson, J and Robertson, J (1952) *A Two-Year-Old Goes to Hospital*. Robertson Films.

Rustin, M (2009) Esther Bick's Legacy of Infant Observation at the Tavistock: Some Reflections 60 Years On. *Infant Observation*, 12(1): 29–41.

Sheridan, M, Sharma, A and Cockerill, H (2007) *From Birth to Five Years: Children's Developmental Progress*. Abingdon: Routledge.

Sylva, K, Roy, C and Painter, M (1980) *Childwatching at Playgroup and Nursery School*. London: Grant McIntyre.

Taylor, C (2004) Underpinning Knowledge for Child Care Practice: Reconsidering Child Development Theory. *Child and Family Social Work*, 9: 225–35.

Trowell, J and Miles, G (1991) The Contribution of Observation Training to Professional Development in Social Work. *Journal of Social Work Practice*, 5(1): 51–60.

United Nations (1989) *United Nations Convention on the Rights of the Child*. New York: United Nations.

3 Developing skills in observation

Objectives

This chapter will enable you to:

- reflect on issues in your own life that affect your ability to observe;
- identify and begin to develop the skills needed to observe;
- consider the impact of your presence on the child and their carers;
- negotiate your role and place as an observer;
- record observations effectively.

Introduction

We see things not as they are, but as we are.

(Immanuel Kant, 1724–1804)

We can only see what fits into our mental space, and all description includes interpretation as well as sensory reporting.

(Angrosino 2005: 743)

The first quotation is from the German philosopher Immanuel Kant and is cited in the final overview report into the death of Daniel Pelka (Coventry LSCB 2013: 71). The second is taken from a discussion about the role of observation in ethnographic research. These quotations reflect a recognition of the deeply subjective nature of all observation and of the central difficulty referred to in the Introduction of trying to understand the limitations of our own view, in order to see things as they really are.

The focus in this chapter is solely on a holistic, experiential approach to observation, which is seen as of particular value in understanding children, their emotions and their relationships with others. It is recognised that in many instances practitioners will also be listening, talking and interacting, but in order to integrate observation effectively into our practice, it is helpful first to focus on the process and skills needed to observe. Chapter 4 will then provide examples of the application of observation skills in practice settings and the supporting conversations that may helpfully accompany observation, particularly with children and young people who are able to express themselves verbally.

Skills in observing experientially are usually learned and developed through engaging in an extended observation study of an infant or young child. Typically, this would be for one hour per week, for anything from six weeks to one year. The observations are written up afterwards, but ideally on the same day, with observers encouraged to use a free-flowing 'stream of consciousness' style, that includes what they have observed, what they perceived of the feelings and mood of the observed, as well as any apparently random thoughts, flashbacks and their own feelings. These are explored in a small seminar group, which provides an opportunity for participants to reflect and challenge each other, questioning perceptions, interpretations, emphases, omissions and value judgements. Invariably participants find that they are reminded of experiences in their childhood which are forming unconscious reference points, or they are perhaps comparing what is happening with their own experience of being a parent.

The seminar group provides a supportive context in which the participants can become conscious of and think about the many aspects of their own experience that impact on receptivity, perception and interpretation of what is noticed or *seen*. It is also helpful if this is accompanied by input on theory, which informs the subsequent analysis of the subject of the observation study.

However, few students and practitioners currently have the opportunity to participate in this type of small-group learning. While this chapter cannot be a substitute for the rich learning that such participation can provide, it attempts to guide the reader and provide activities that will enhance the development of skills in observation, prompting some similar opportunities for reflection and learning to those outlined above, as well as supporting those who are currently participating in child observation studies. Hopefully it will also create a thirst to participate in further professional development in this area.

Receptivity: a prerequisite for observers

Developments in neuroscience have led to a much greater understanding of the role of sensory perception in understanding. It is now recognised that there are many more senses than those traditionally identified by Aristotle, as well as the physiological responses triggered by emotions, for example the *fight or flight* response to fear. Thiele in Munro (2011: 37) explains that:

> It is estimated that our sense organs collect between 200,000 and 1 million bits of information for every bit of information that enters our conscious awareness. Conscious perception represents only the smallest fraction of what we absorb from our worldly encounters.

An important starting point for observers is thus to recognise the role of sensory perception in gathering information and to consciously practise using our senses, so that we become more confident in using data that we have gathered in this way.

Observation involves the attunement of our senses to what is happening around us. Think for a moment about a cat that has smelt a possible predator, or prey: the body is still, motionless, but poised, the head up and alert, eyes wide, ears pricked up, so that it is receptive to information from all its senses. It will feel the breeze (touch), sensing where the wind is coming from, it will smell the scent, listen to hear any sounds and search for the smallest movement with its eyes. Here the cat is using four of the five senses traditionally identified by Aristotle: sight, hearing, touch, smell and taste.

Activity

Pause for a moment while you are reading and try to adopt the alert physical posture described above. Do this for a minute and see what you have noticed that you were not previously aware of.

Practise this twice a day, in different settings, adopting the physically alert stance outlined above, for two minutes. Afterwards write down everything you became aware of. A useful structure to begin with might be to use the traditional five senses as headings, plus 'feelings' to capture anything else that you have sensed, but find harder to locate.

Keeping a log for one week of the information that you have gathered in this way will enable you to see any changes in your perception over this time.

COMMENT

We could call this listening with our bodies, being open to a range of information that may otherwise become lost in the focus on words and content. It requires intense, focused concentration. The observer is not passive, but alert and still. Thinking about the information we receive through our senses also encourages us to be more conscious of the information conveyed through the bodies of those we are observing, so we learn to 'listen' to their facial expressions and bodies as well as their words. This heightened level of receptivity may enable us to notice uncomfortable feelings that we cannot quite locate. These need to be held on to and thought about.

While we may be attuned to thinking about some aspects of non-verbal communication, such as whether the body posture is open or closed, it is also helpful to observe and give conscious attention to movement, or indeed the absence of movement, particularly in children, as this can tell us a great deal about their health, happiness and well-being. In children of two to five years old, bursts of energy, often running rather than walking, are usually interspersed with periods of quieter play, so when we see children who are still, watching their carers before moving, we need to be professionally curious about the reason for this.

In relation to Daniel Pelka, referred to in the first chapter, his observed behaviour was very unusual. Young children who have just started school more typically scan eagerly for their parents/carers and run out to greet them, showing pleasure in being reunited with a significant attachment figure and enjoying the freedom to run about. Hence in the context of other information that was known, Daniel's behaviour was certainly unusual and worthy of further exploration. Similarly his mother's physical distance from Daniel sends powerful messages about her relationship with him.

Perception

Perception refers to *'the ability to see, hear or become aware of something through the senses'* (Concise Oxford English Dictionary). Each individual will perceive things in their own unique way, influenced by a range of factors. One of the difficulties associated with using information gathered through our senses is that of knowing how our sensory perception is affected by our own personal experience, likes and dislikes, as well as our gender, class, ethnicity and culture. The following list is a helpful starting point in drawing our attention to some of the contextual issues that will inform what we see, when we observe:

*   physical appearance of the child we are observing;

*   behaviour of the child;

*   knowledge of the child's culture;

*   beliefs and values from our own parenting or experience of friends' and relatives' children;

*   our own childhood experience, both in the home and at school;

*   professional training and value base;

*   reason for the observation;

*   state of mind (tired, preoccupied, etc.).

Activity

Spend five minutes watching a video clip of a baby or child with their family. You can find many useful examples on YouTube (www.youtube.com) if you enter a search term such as 'super nanny', 'happy toddlers eating well' or 'toddler tantrums'. These will elicit a range of conscious and unconscious responses within you.

Return to the list above and consider the influence of these factors on your perception.

COMMENT

As I watched some American clips on YouTube, such as 'Monica eats pop rocks', I was very aware of the impact of my own views about the (American) food industry and the way I perceive this as impacting on the well-being of children such as Monica, which in turn impacts on how I then interpreted what I observed. Watching Piper in '2 year old devastated about new born sister' by Rumble Viral, I felt an unsettling sense of inner distress as I observed her palpable sense of being abandoned and what appeared to me to be a deeply insensitive response by her father.

Your responses to this material may be different from mine. There is no right or wrong response, the important thing is to be aware of your responses and recognise the impact they have on your perception. If you are able to complete this activity with a colleague, it may be valuable to compare your perceptions and explore the factors that have influenced this. When a similar exercise is undertaken with students who are preparing to undertake observations, they are often surprised by their widely differing perceptions of what they have seen.

Interpretation

Differences in receptivity and perception are necessarily followed by differences in interpretation. As we have seen, there is always a significant degree of subjectivity in what we perceive or pay attention to, whether through our senses or in conversation, so absolute objectivity is unattainable. However, as a step towards clarifying our understanding of what we are observing, it is helpful to recognise whether we are responding to something that is coming from the child and their environment or whether our response to what we have observed is coming from our own experience and biases. Trowell and Miles (1991: 53) suggest that the ability to do this is central to the whole process of observation. They explain that observers need

> to be aware of their own responses as a source of invaluable data, provided they are aware of what comes from them and what comes from their clients, and to develop the capacity to integrate these.

A helpful illustration of this was given by a social worker on a post-qualifying course who was undertaking a child observation module, in addition to her demanding caseload. Before presenting her observation to the seminar group she explained that she had been feeling tired, so was not looking forward to another visit and had considered cancelling her observation, which was due to take place after she finished work. She explained that she was very glad that she had not cancelled it: she observed a bath time with both parents and their two-year-old child. The house was warm, the family was relaxed and she observed a great deal of laughter and reciprocal play. When asked about her mood at the end of the observation she commented that it was interesting that she felt happy and no longer felt tired.

COMMENT

In this example the social worker was able to reflect on her feelings prior to the visit and rec-ognise that her reluctance and weariness came from her feelings about visiting families on her caseload where she was experiencing considerable apprehension about what she might encounter (so something that she was carrying that came with her). The happiness that she felt came from the child. The shift in her mood told her something about what it was like to be in the home she was visiting and to be a child in that household.

Preparing to observe

The first issue for many observers, who are used to always being busy, active and having something to *do* or a task to complete, is to think about how it feels to be an observer, where we are not having to *do*, but rather to *be*. It can be difficult to be still. Working out where to look, if you are not engaged in conversation, can also be tricky. For many people, a direct gaze feels uncomfortable, especially if they have grown up in a culture where it is considered rude to stare.

Activity

What are you usually doing when you are with children? How does it feel to put all of that on one side?

Or, is it rare for you to be able to spend time with children? Do you feel worried that you know very little about young children and perhaps feel uncomfortable in their presence?

COMMENT

Whatever our starting point, it is important to reflect on this and to be aware of the impact it may have. If we are able to reflect on these feelings, why we have them and where they come from, we are more likely to be able to be fully present and open to what we are observing. If we personally feel uncomfortable about being with children or about our roles as observers, we may find ourselves unconsciously sabotaging the process, either by not making the time to do it as there are always competing priorities for our time, or by not being emotionally pre-sent and therefore unable to receive anything when we do observe.

Observers who are not parents may worry about their ability to observe, but within my own experience of participating in an observation seminar group, I have noticed that those of us who are parents sometimes have more difficulty in thinking about the experience of the child, as we readily identify with the parent, perhaps thinking about our own parenting and comparing that with the parenting that we are observing. Those who are not parents are sometimes very sensitive to what is happening for the child, but may be more reticent about voicing opinions.

Observers may face many different sources of anxiety as they prepare to observe. They may feel anxious about being an observer, about the particular child and about those who are caring for the child. The context for the observation may also be a source of concern, as may other people who might be present and the physical location. These anxieties have the potential to block receptivity and therefore it is important to attend to them.

Activity

Imagine that you need to ask a family you are working with if you can observe them for an hour as part of your work with them.

What issues would there be for you? Using the headings suggested below explore your feelings about:

- *being an observer;*
- *the child you are observing;*
- *the family and environment.*

An example of the issues that could come up might look like this:

Feelings about being an observer	Feelings about the child you are observing	Feelings about the family and environment
I feel awkward just sitting there. I will seem useless. I haven't got time for this. What will I tell my manager I did? How will I cope if she screams? I'm black and male –everyone else there is white and female.	She's always very lively and exhausting. I don't know how I would cope with her. She reminds me of … I feel sad mine are grown up now … I'd like to take her home with me, I feel so sorry for her.	I'm scared of their dog. I feel sorry for Mum, she's trying really hard. There is a weird smell in the house. The television is always on and really loud.

Figure 3.1 *Preparing to observe: identifying feelings*

COMMENT

All the above comments are derived from concerns that have been shared by students and practitioners participating in observation seminar groups. They reflect some of the wide range of issues relating to our identity, self-esteem and experience, as well as the impact of the context, which may all have a bearing on our perception and ability to observe. These issues may distract or distort our ability to be fully present and to attend to the child's experience.

If, for example, a child stirs powerful memories of a younger sibling, 'she reminded me of my sister – a spoiled brat', it may be hard to fully engage with the experience of the actual child that you are observing. Awareness of and conscious attention to these difficulties may help us begin to understand the possible impact on our understanding and our ability to observe.

Writing honestly about how we are feeling can provide a very helpful, private space for reflection and processing our feelings. It has the advantage that we can throw the pages away when we have worked through our feelings! Alternatively, peer supervision or line management supervision, if available, can provide a very helpful space to discuss such issues.

Epoché and bracketing

Phenomenological research is a qualitative research method originating from German philosophy. The task of the qualitative researcher undertaking this type of research is to understand the central essence or meaning of lived experience (Romanyshyn 2007). Hence, there are useful parallels here with the task of social workers, who are attempting to understand the lived experience of the children and families they are working with. So it is worthwhile considering how phenomenological researchers endeavour to deal with some of the difficulties outlined so far in this chapter, particularly in relation to perception and interpretation. The concepts of *epoché* and *bracketing* are of particular interest.

The term *epoché* is used to describe the phase during which the researcher '*attends to experience*' (Romanyshyn 2007: 149), identifying anything within their personal experience that resonates or connects with the situation being studied, in order to recognise preconceptions they may have about the situation, becoming aware of any '*prejudices, viewpoints or assumptions*' that have a bearing on this.

The notion of *bracketing* follows this, suggesting that we then attempt to contain those issues we have become aware of and, quite literally, put a bracket around them (Denzin and Lincoln 2003: 217). In practice this is not a neat and tidy process and indeed may never be fully achieved, but nevertheless the discipline of asking ourselves the following questions as we prepare to observe may be helpful:

»	*What in my own life connects with or has a bearing on what I am going to observe?*
»	*How best can I put brackets around these in order to be fully present?*
»	*How may my view still be affected?*

Figure 3.2 *Preparing to observe: attending to previous experience*

The following extract from an essay on observation helps to illustrate this process in action.

> *I was observing Jacob (age three) playing in the nursery garden with a small hard rubber quoit. He was throwing the quoit up into the tree and was busily running*

around, picking it up and throwing it back into the tree. Three little girls then also started to play under the tree. Jacob was enthusiastically carrying on with his game when eventually the quoit landed on top of one of the little girls. This made her cry, which attracted the attention of one of the staff, who then asked Jacob to apologise to the child who was hurt. He was looking around trying to see where his quoit was. He pointed at it and tried to go and get it. However, the staff member was holding on to him and trying to make him say sorry. Jacob was looking in the other direction when the quoit hit the girl, so I don't think he understood the connection between throwing the quoit and the injury to the little girl. He looked bewildered and became very upset. Eventually he cried, but did not say sorry.

I found this very difficult to observe as it connected directly with my own experience as a child which came flooding back to me. I was always getting the blame for everything that went wrong, so I felt the injustice of it very strongly. I felt vulnerable and I know I tend to see all children as helpless and vulnerable.

I recognised that I needed to set my experience aside, to put a bracket around it, and see Jacob's experience for what it was, rather than through the lens of my own experience. However, I think I had a heightened awareness of the impact that a very small event, such as this, can have on a young child.

Activity

Waiting for a bus or train or queuing at a supermarket checkout both provide excellent opportunities for inconspicuous observation. Practising the alert stance identified above, consciously observe what is happening. Afterwards write down what you observed and then answer the three questions above.

COMMENT

Initially the very focused concentration required and the disciplined process of teasing out the issues that influence you is very difficult, but with practice and, if available, the support of colleagues, it can become a way of being that you can consciously switch into.

A quiet self is needed in order to be present. A troubled or distracted self will struggle to take anything else in. Perhaps this is one reason why sometimes it is a relief not to succeed in gaining access to observe.

Negotiating the role with others

Having considered some of the steps needed to prepare ourselves to observe, it is important to focus on how others may feel about being observed and to recognise the impact that this may have on them. We need to explain the role of the observer and the purpose of observation in order to negotiate our presence with the child, the family and anyone else who may be present or have an interest.

The starting point is always to ensure that practice is consistent with social work values. There is a need to be open and transparent, recognising the impact of power relationships and diversity. Le Riche and Tanner (1998) suggest that a '*power lens*' may enable us to develop an equality model of observation. It is not always easy for practitioners to recognise their own power, as they may feel anxious and have little power within their own organisation. Nevertheless, in relation to service users there are always significant inequalities that need to be recognised in any negotiation.

As part of the process of seeking agreement it is important to fully discuss all aspects and stages of the observations. Will you follow them around, and if so, what are the limits to this? Privacy needs to be respected, as does the right of the child and the carers to say *no*, they do not want you to observe (though there may be some exceptions to this which will be referred in the next chapter). In practice children are more often delighted that someone is interested in their world and may be relieved that they are not going to be asked any questions. Parents and carers may understandably be more wary, given the many complex and ambiguous expectations of parents and the role of social workers, as often portrayed by the media.

Figure 3.3 (based on Ellis et al 1998) below, provides a possible format for a written agreement that includes consent, as well as clarifying the details of what will be happening. This could be adapted in discussion with the child and carers to address the particular context and issues that arise in the process of negotiation.

Explaining observation to children and seeking consent/assent

As we saw in previous chapters, the Children Act (1989), the UNCRC, case law (Gillick competency) and the Professional Capabilities Framework (2012) provide a context which requires a considered approach to seeking informed consent to observation. However, in practice, views differ widely according to professional backgrounds and settings in relation to whether this is seen as necessary and to the approach that is taken. If we adopt an approach informed by a recognition of the competence of children and young people and a commitment to respecting them, we need to give careful thought to how we discuss observation with them. With very young children and babies we need to discuss with their parents how best to undertake the observations and, where appropriate, explain our presence and role in a way that will be helpful and appropriate for their child.

Activity (a)

How would you approach a situation where you are undertaking an assessment in relation to a young person aged 13 who is the subject of a Care Order (Children Act 1989, section 31) but has returned to live at home with her parents? Her parents have given consent, but she has not. Is her consent required?

An agreement between:

Name of child to be observed

Name(s) of parent(s) of child to be observed

Name of observer

Name(s) of staff representing nursery/playgroup/other care

Period of observation: from ....

                                    to   ....

Times of observations   ....

Agreed locations   ....

Terms of agreement

(1) Eastshire Children's Services confirms that ....(name of observer) is a registered/qualified social worker who will undertake the task of observing a child for one hour per week for .... weeks, commencing on .... and ending on ....

(2) Greta Jones (Team Manager) from Eastshire Children's Services can be contacted on 0000 XXXX if you have any concerns about the observations that cannot be discussed directly with your social worker.

(3) Eastshire Children's Services will stop the observations at the request of the child/young person/ parent/carer of the observed child and/or on the recommendation of the day care facility where appropriate.

(4) Agreed purpose of the observations:

(5) The observer has explained to .... (the child/young person) why they want to observe (and .... has agreed to this)*

(6) The parent/carer agrees that .... (name of observer) may observe .... (name of child) for one hour per week for .... weeks.

(7) The observer will record what they have observed within 24 hours of the observation taking place.

(8) Access to observation recordings is restricted to .... (those observed), the observer, team manager and other members of the Core Group with responsibility for ....

(9) The observer agrees to attend the place of observation only at the arranged times and to inform the child/young person, child's parent(s) and/or carers if they are unable to attend at any time.

SIGNATURES: ....

....

DATE ....

(name and role in relation to child or organisation should be printed alongside signature)

Figure 3.3 Sample observation agreement

COMMENT

This is a difficult situation that requires careful consideration of a range of factors including:

- the paramountcy of the welfare of the child;

- the parental responsibility of the Local Authority (the parents have not ceased to have parental responsibility, although they cannot exercise this in a way that interferes with the Local Authority plans);

- whether the young person is of sufficient age and understanding *to be capable of making up (her or his) own mind on the matter requiring decision* (see above, p. 39).

Activity (b)

Think of a way you might ask a child aged two for assent to observe?

How might you explain to the child your purpose and role as an observer?

COMMENT

Examples from students undertaking observations of young children as part of their training include:

It's a long time since I was two, so I would like to spend some time at your house remembering what it's like to be two.

With a three-and-a-half-year-old child who has an older sibling:

I go to big school called university. One of the things my teacher wants me to do is learn about being three years old, so is it alright if I sit over here, or is there a better place for me to be? ... My teacher says I can't join in, I just need to sit quietly.

Other students have tried asking if they can learn about how a child plays, but have found this problematic, as the child may then feel they have to endlessly assemble jigsaws, build towers, etc.! Furthermore, it does not accurately reflect the task of the observer.

Activity (c)

What difference does the child's age make to your feelings about consulting children?

How would you decide who you would talk to first, the child or the parent?

Finding a way of introducing yourself that feels authentic and works for you will take time and will be dependent on the age and understanding of the child and the purpose of your observation. The impact of power, discussed above in relation to negotiating the role, as in all aspects of social work practice, needs to be addressed and will be explored further in the next chapter.

The explanation needs to include discussion about the purpose of the observation, when and what you will record and who this will be shared with. Within an educational context, where much of the recording will focus on the learning and reflection for the observer, this focus has sometimes been used as a reason for not sharing the recording with the subjects of the observation. However, given that the focus of the observation is also the child and their interaction with those around them, it is difficult to argue that this position is consistent with the principles of openness and transparency. A way forward may be to agree with the observed what will be written up and shared and to explain that you will also be keeping a personal learning log, which contains your personal thoughts and feelings, following your observation.

We also need to be very careful and sensitive to a child's wish to subsequently change their mind, particularly in relation to any recordings of the observations and what should happen to them, recognising that they may later withdraw consent. Agreement therefore needs to be regularly reviewed by the observer during and after the observations. If, for example, a young child shows embarrassment, distress or discomfort because of the presence of the observer it would be right for the observer to end the observation.

While the process of negotiation and agreement will have set out the structure for the observations, at the beginning of each observation there is a need to ensure that everyone is as comfortable as possible about your presence, before settling in to the observer role. Using the skills that you would use in any other context to put others at ease and engaging in the usual social exchanges can be helpful. Jordan (1990, p 179) wrote about the importance of 'ordinariness in unordinary situations', a helpful reminder of the need always to be real, to be authentic and to recognise our common humanity.

Activity

What does the notion of being ordinary mean for you as a practitioner? How might it affect the way you introduce yourself to those you are observing? Consider this in relation to:

- *a young person aged 14;*
- *a father/mother/carer.*

COMMENT

The processes of negotiating your role and introduction will take practice. Those you are observing will not be able to relax if you are tense. Similarly, if the worries of those being observed have not been satisfactorily addressed they will feel unable to continue with their activities or to accept you as an observer. As was discussed in the previous chapter, your presence will always have an impact, which needs to be recognised and reflected upon. You are necessarily a participant observer, but the aim should be to minimise your interference with what is happening.

Doing observations

The preparations suggested above may provide a helpful starting point for undertaking observations. Essentially the task may then appear straightforward and entails:

- observing the child intently and their interactions with those around them;

- responding to interaction but not initiating ... a participant observer;

- being aware of the impact of the environment;

- producing a detailed record of the observation and the thoughts and feelings that this evoked.

In reality these tasks are very challenging. Some of the reasons for this have already been referred to above, in terms of context and the personal experiences and feelings that the observer brings. We also need to think about what is happening, and what needs to happen, beneath the surface during the process of observation. According to Miller et al (1989, p 7):

> [T]he practice of systematic observation of the development of infants provides the observer with an opportunity to observe **primitive emotional states** in the infant and his family and indeed in the observer's own response to the turbulent environment.

This quotation helps us to understand why observers who are attuned to the child are often taken aback by the emotional intensity of the experience when they observe, both in relation to their awareness of the child's experience and in relation to the powerful, long-forgotten memories that may come flooding into the observer's consciousness, as in the example of the observation of Jacob earlier in this chapter.

Maintaining the observer stance also entails relinquishing a degree of control of the situation. The observer needs to patiently follow unfolding events. This can feel time-consuming, mundane and boring and it may seem unlikely to answer the particular questions that we are seeking answers to. The urgency of competing priorities in our lives will be pressing when watching, for example, a five-month-old baby repeatedly reaching out (and failing) to grasp an object. It may be for five minutes, but may feel like an eternity! But from this we may learn about the availability of a supporting environment, both physically and emotionally, the capacity of the carer/s to support the child's development, the persistence and drive of the baby, as well as the order of her day.

In the following example from a colleague, this 11-month-old baby's reaction to momentary separation in the presence of a stranger/observer reveals something about the nature of his attachment relationship with his mother.

> His mum attempted to sit him down on the floor, placing several toys in front of him, so that she could go into the kitchen and put the kettle on. As soon as she moved out of sight he began to whimper. His mum put her head round the door and said, 'It's all right, I'm here'. He gave a slight sigh, then started to crawl towards her. As soon as he could see her he stopped and remained where he was. When she came back into the room she picked him up and sat him on her lap, but he wriggled to get down again!

This observer had commented on a number of occasions on the tedium of the observations, but recognised on reflection that in the mundane ordinariness of everyday life, she had learned a great deal about this baby's experience and his mother's responsiveness, as well as learning about her own ability to be still and receptive.

The requirement to stay with uncertainty and 'suspend judgement' (Trowell and Miles 1991) referred to in the previous chapter also poses challenges, as this runs counter to the usual constant filtering, ordering and processing of messages received through our senses. However, the struggle to stay with uncertainty, recognising the limitations of our knowledge, is important as it encourages observers to stay in the present and to remain open to what is happening, rather than forming an immediate view about whether something is satisfactory. In our daily lives we tend to form impressions very quickly and then interpret or filter subsequent information in the light of that impression, which can mean that insufficient attention is paid to information that does not fit with our view of how things are.

This point is also pertinent to the difficulty that can arise in situations where practitioners are reassured by seeing a positive interaction between a child and carers, as, for example, in the case of Kimberley Carlile, where the social worker's anxieties were allayed when he saw the whole family together, apparently interacting in a positive way. The report comments:

> Those working in the field of child abuse must always be on their guard against the risk of seeing what they want to believe.
>
> (London Borough of Greenwich 1987, p 112)

In this instance the formation of a premature view resulted in less attention being given to the information that was concerning, which was then reinterpreted in the light of the reassuring encounter.

Staying open can mean being in touch with the unbearable reality of the child's experience. While this chapter can help you to be more aware of the need to recognise and stay with difficult uncertainties, good supervision is vital in order to be able to face them and work effectively.

Staying focused on the child while observing is also challenging, sometimes because the detail of a child's play may be repetitive and it is easy to lose focus or think that we have seen what we need to see. At other times the overwhelming needs of other adults and children can make this very difficult, particularly in a chaotic household or a busy day-care setting. The neglected child's presence may be marked by an absence from view. So while an awareness of the whole context is important, including awareness of those who are interacting with the child, it is essential that the prime focus is always on the child who is the identified focus of your practice.

When is intervention needed?

The question of what to do if something is observed that may cause harm to a child is often asked in discussions about child observation. In practice, observers respond intuitively to physical harm, rightly intervening if something may cause immediate injury to a child, such as a baby trapping their fingers in a toy. Emotionally abusive encounters where children are shouted at and criticised may require a different approach, where there is a difficult balance to be maintained between gaining an insight into the established pattern of interaction in the family, providing feedback to the abusive parent and ensuring that the observer is not seen by the child to collude with the abusive behaviour.

Recording

When using this holistic experiential approach observers are strongly advised to record after the observation, rather than during it. If observers avert their gaze to record while they are observing, they will miss many signals that comprise part of the experience of the child. This may feel less uncomfortable for the observer, as it lessens the emotional intensity of the experience, enabling the observer to disengage while recording. Observers often feel anxious that they will forget, but with practice recall improves swiftly. There will, however, be times when, for you as a social worker, the observation has a particular purpose (eg to record the frequency of a particular behaviour) or to obtain and record pieces of information, where it may be more appropriate to adopt a different approach to observation and recording, as outlined in the previous chapter.

It is, however, always important to record as soon as possible *after* the observation for two closely related reasons. Accurate and detailed recall fades very quickly and any information received through the senses may swiftly be reinterpreted in the light of ongoing daily activities. Hence, anything that has been observed that subsequently needs to be used for evidence in any court proceedings will not be considered to be reliable if it is not recorded as soon as reasonably practicable. Figure 3.4 provides an overview of the Family Court rules of evidence, which it is helpful to be mindful of.

Recordings need to include:

• the interaction that has been observed in chronological order and sequence, as a free-flowing narrative;

• the emotional state (mood) of the child as perceived by the observer;

• the observer's own responses (including feelings) in the situation.

High-quality recording may ensure that there is sufficient evidence to make decisions and to take action to safeguard children if it is needed at a later date. Key points are as follows:

Notes should be made contemporaneously. This is defined as **an accurate record, made at the time, or as soon after the event as practicable**. It is a record of relevant evidence which has been seen, heard or done, by the maker of the record.

Recordings that are not made within twenty-four hours will not be considered reliable, regardless of whether a weekend or Bank Holiday has followed the observation. Recordings made immediately after the event will have greater weight placed on them than those made a few hours later.

Original notes, whether typed or handwritten, need to be retained, dated and signed.

Courts may ask to see any records that you wish to rely upon as evidence, so always be mindful of this.

The law makes a clear distinction between facts and opinion, although in reality they are not opposites, but need to be seen as existing on a continuum. Facts provide best evidence and only facts are admissible as evidence. However, professionals are able to express opinions in areas where they can demonstrate professional expertise, either as an aspect of competence intrinsic to their profession, or arising from particular training that they have undertaken. Nevertheless, greater weight will normally still be placed on any factual evidence.

There is a particular skill entailed in learning to record in a more factual way, which can be helped by developing skills in detailed observations, as careful observations provide more factual information. For example, '*she seemed drunk*' is an opinion based on a value judgement which only a medically qualified practitioner could express. However, a recording that describes what the person was doing that made the writer form that impression, provides more factual evidence, as in the following example:

> *She was shouting loudly, but her speech was unclear so I could not understand what was being said: usually she speaks quietly and clearly. When she stood up she swayed unsteadily and bumped into the furniture as she moved about. There was a smell of stale beer and empty beer cans and empty wine bottles on the floor.*

Initially this way of recording may feel unnecessarily laborious. We are more used to summarising information that we have observed and making value judgements as a quick way of conveying meaning.

In another example, if we return to the recollection of the teaching assistant in relation to Daniel Pelka's mother – '*Ms Luczak always seemed cross with him*' – this is recorded as an opinion. There is some detail that supports this opinion, '*He always walked twenty paces behind his mother*', but further detail would strengthen this statement and move this towards a more factual statement that could be used as evidence. So, for example, it might include, '*I never saw his mother smile at him. She frowned at him and I frequently heard her telling him off, or criticising him. Examples of this included telling him off for spilling food on his clothing, for being slow coming out of school and making her wait, for scuffing his shoes and for looking untidy with his shirt hanging out.*'

So, developing good skills in observation will enable you to develop a disciplined approach to recording and presenting information more effectively in formal contexts where evidence for your views is required.

Figure 3.4 *Rules of evidence: Family Court proceedings*

Personal reflection on the observation will include such things as:

- What effect might the observation have had on the child/carers?
- What were you feeling at the time?
- What are you feeling now?
- What in my own life connected with what I observed?
- How have I addressed that (bracketing)?
- How may my view still be affected?
- What do I know from theory and research that has a bearing on what I have observed?

This approach enables the observer to separate out the content of the recording, so that it can be shared with those being observed, from some of the personal reflection which might be more appropriately shared in supervision and used as part of the ongoing process of making sense of the child's experience.

The place of observation in understanding children's experience

Holistic, experiential observations can provide a valuable source of information about a child and their situation, but they also have significant limitations. As we have seen, they are necessarily subjective, as all information within them is mediated by the limits of the observer's skills and their own personal and professional experience. Observations may give rise to many more questions which cannot be answered by simply observing but require further sources of information in order to find answers. Information from observations therefore needs to be placed within a wider framework as shown in figure 3.5 below in order to maximise its effectiveness. Drawing on qualitative research methods, it is helpful always to consider how we can triangulate any tentative findings. First, wherever possible, it is important to seek to listen to the views of those who have been observed, however partial those views may be. The following may provide a useful mental checklist.

- What can we learn from the child (through observation and conversations)?
- What can we learn from others: the family, carers and professionals who know the child (through observation and conversations)?
- What do we know about the context?
- What written sources of information are there (case files, reports)?
- How can relevant theory, research into practice (Serious Case Reviews, policy reviews), etc. inform our understanding of what we see?

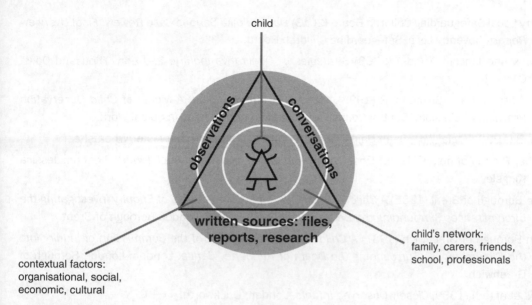

Figure 3.5 Contextualising information from observations

Conclusion

In this chapter the processes and skills involved in observing have been separated out from those needed to listen and communicate, in order to support the development of skills in what may initially feel an unnatural activity. It has highlighted the importance of self-awareness, being receptive and staying open, adopting a *not knowing* approach. As we have seen, the emotional intensity, discomfort and periodic boredom create challenges that may discourage observers from persevering with this way of understanding the lives of those with whom they are working. However, the insights that observation can provide make this approach an invaluable addition to the skills that practitioners can draw on, not only as part of the process of assessment, but also as a method of intervention, as illustrated in the next chapter.

Taking it further

Baldwin, M (1994) Why Observe Children?, *Social Work Education*, 13(2): 74–85.

O'Loughlin, M and O'Loughlin, S (2014) *Effective Observation in Social Work Practice*. London: Sage.

Simonetta, M, Adamo, G and Rustin, M (eds) (2014) *Young Child Observation: A Development in the Method of Infant Observation*. London: Karnac.

Trowell, J and Miles, G (1991) The Contribution of Observation Training to Professional Development in Social Work. *Journal of Social Work Practice*, 5(1): 51–60.

References

Angrosino, M (2005) Recontextualising Observation, in Denzin, N and Lincoln, Y (eds) *The Sage Handbook of Qualitative Research*, 3rd edn. Thousand Oaks, CA: Sage.

Coventry Local Safeguarding Children Board (2013) *Daniel Pelka Serious Case Review: Final Overview Report*. Coventry Local Safeguarding Children Board.

Denzin, N and Lincoln, Y (eds) (2003) *Strategies of Qualitative Inquiry*, 2nd edn. Thousand Oaks, CA: Sage.

Ellis, L, Lasson, I and Solomon, R (1998) *Keeping Children in Mind: A Model of Child Observation Practice*. Chelmsford: Central Council for Education and Training in Social Work.

Jordan, B (1990) *Social Work in an Unjust Society*. Hemel Hempstead: Harvester Wheatsheaf.

Le Riche, P and Tanner, K (1998) *Observation and its Application to Social Work*. London: Jessica Kingsley.

London Borough of Brent (1985) *A Child in Trust: The Report of the Panel of Enquiry Investigating the Circumstances Surrounding the Death of Jasmine Beckford*. London Borough of Brent.

London Borough of Greenwich (1987) *A Child in Mind: The Report of the Commission of Inquiry into the Circumstances Surrounding the Death of Kimberley Carlile*. London: London Borough of Greenwich.

Miller, L et al (ed) (1989) *Closely Observed Infants*. London: Duckworth.

Munro, E (2011) *Munro Review of Child Protection: Interim Report: The Child's Journey*, DFE-00010-2011. London: Department for Education, www.gov.uk/government/collections/munro-review (accessed 22 September 2015).

Romanyshyn, R D (2007) *The Wounded Researcher: Research with the Soul in Mind*. New Orleans: Spring Journal Books.

Thiele, L P (2006) *The Heart of Judgement: Practical Wisdom, Neuroscience, and Narrative*. New York: Cambridge University Press.

Trowell, J and Miles, G (1991) The Contribution of Observation Training to Professional Development in Social Work. *Journal of Social Work Practice*, 5(1): 51–60.

4 Using observation in practice

Objectives

This chapter will:

- explore key issues that shape the practice of observation: identity, power, previous experience and context;

- consider what social workers mean by *observation*;

- provide examples of the use of observation in a range of practice settings with children and families;

- explore the process of reflecting on and deriving meaning from observations.

Introduction

Observation is the only true way to ever get a sense of what's going on. People can tell you what they like!

While all practitioners see observation as something that is part of the social work role, views vary widely about what they mean by observation, what it entails and whether it is feasible to incorporate observation into social work practice. Some, as in the quotation given above, regard it as vital, 'It's not just possible, it's essential', whereas others feel that it is a luxury, 'almost soft', something which may be hard to justify where there are resource constraints and too little time.

Views may be shaped by previous training and experience, as well as the organisational context and culture. They may also be influenced by some of the literature on infant observation, which, as we saw in Chapter 2, requires the observer to remain entirely detached from the interaction that they are observing in order both to minimise their impact on the observed and to maintain the intense concentration and focus that is needed if they are to be fully present and alert to what is happening in the room. While this optimises what can be learned from the experience of observing, it may leave practitioners feeling that this approach to observation is of limited use in practice, as they cannot just observe; they need and want to engage with children and families, conduct assessments, gather information and find solutions to the difficulties that children and families are facing.

However, more recent work has suggested that there is a way forward. This has challenged the view of non-participant infant observation as providing the 'gold standard' for observation and recognises that when observing children, young people and families, some degree of participation can be entirely appropriate and indeed helpful (Simonetta et al 2014). This work is helpful in legitimising the pragmatic solutions that many practitioners have found, but had thought were perhaps less than the ideal to which their training suggested they should aspire.

This chapter will first explore some of the wider issues that influence the process and practice of observation and then provide examples from practitioners that illustrate the ways in which observation can make a valuable contribution to the practice of social workers and other professionals working with children and families.

Issues that shape the process of observation

Identity

How we identify ourselves, personally and professionally, will have an impact on our views about observation. The respective identities of the observer and the observed therefore need careful consideration, as both bring narratives to the encounter that will shape what it is possible to see and how that can be thought about. According to Lawler (2014) identity may be said to include the broad social categories such as ethnicity, class, gender, sexuality, disability, as well as our lived subjective experience, our *felt* identity, hence it is not fixed, but evolves over time. She argues that the relationship between the social categories available to us and the ways in which we can then live and understand our lives is central to understanding identity (Lawler 2014: 9). Social categories thus inform others' views of who we are and also shape our own sense of who we are.

Social categories confer power and are imbued with values, conveying taken-for-granted norms about what constitutes the 'right' way of doing things. Social workers may feel powerless and may indeed at times be vulnerable, but to those they are working with they are powerful and could be threatening. For a child, this may be by virtue of age alone, but may also include other aspects of identity which the child may attribute to them – parent, posh, white, old, social worker, etc.

We may not consciously think about the impact of our identity on others, or on what we expect to see, until we are faced with a situation where we feel uncomfortable or become aware that something conflicts with our taken-for-granted norms and values.

Activity

In what social categories would you place yourself (for example, professional, BME/white; male/female; working/middle class; parent/child-free)?

For you, what constitutes:

- *good taste?*
- *good behaviour (in children and young people)?*
- *good parenting?*

Which categories would the children and families with whom you work place you in?

How do these affect your expectations of them and their expectations of you?

COMMENT

The impact of power and diversity, of visible and invisible identity, in any observation needs careful consideration. Social workers' own perception of themselves, their *felt* identity, may be different from that attributed to them by those with whom they are working. Many of us will have been in situations at some point in our lives where we have felt powerless. It is useful to reflect on this and think about how we acted when we felt like this, as it can give some insight into the impact that our presence may have on children and families. Le Riche and Tanner (1998: 49) draw attention to the impact of oppression on the lives of those whom we are observing, and on the process of observation with particular reference to '*the interlocking differences of race, class and gender*'. The '*web of oppression*' (Mullaly 2010) provides a helpful approach to thinking about issues of power and powerlessness, both in relation to our own experience and the experience of those we are observing.

Talking with student social workers it is apparent that the significance of class identity in particular may be overlooked. However, it continues to need consideration, as although some may argue for its declining significance, what is considered 'good' and a preferred way of doing things is often closely associated with white, Western, middle-class norms, values and expectations. Exploring the concept of parenting in seminars, what emerges is that ideas about 'good parenting' are often associated with views about how women as mothers are expected to behave. It may not always accord with the participants' own experience of parenting, or of being parented, but nevertheless may form part of our unconscious basis for thinking about what we see when we observe.

Previous experience

While experience is a factor that helps to shape our identity, it is also helpful to separate this out and consider what it means within the process of observation. Depending on their previous experiences, children and families may have all sorts of expectations and fantasies about the observer, the reasons that they are being observed and how the observer may interpret what they have observed.

> *I know she thinks I'm rubbish, just like my parents do.*

Similarly, observers may have expectations and fantasies, shaped by their experiences, about what children and families they are observing may think about them. One social worker described being very scared before he first went to observe a family, saying:

> *I used to dread it and think everyone knows I don't know what I'm doing!*

His positive experiences over time and the support of his manager have developed his confidence in integrating observation into his practice. However, his feelings reflected a common theme of a lack of confidence and feelings of uncertainty about the observer role, which requires the observer to adopt an open and 'not knowing' approach, waiting to see what happens rather than taking the lead, asking questions and essentially setting their own agenda.

Context

Contexts have a significant bearing on the possibilities for and process of observation. The *organisational context* and culture will play a key role in determining whether value is accorded to learning about children's experience and whether the resources and support are available to enable practitioners to think about the meaning of what they are seeing.

Some *practice contexts*, particularly in provider and therapeutic services, may appear to offer more obvious opportunities for observation. However, it was apparent from discussions with social workers that observation was possible in a very wide range of contexts. Some considered that it was essential to book time to undertake observations in home environments as a part of gathering evidence for care proceedings.

Feelings about the *physical context and environment* will also impact on whether we feel keen to spend time in a family home, or approach it with fear and trepidation. We all have particular things that we find difficult and distracting – for me, dogs, rats and particular smells! Or perhaps the family have a history of violence towards professionals and you find them intimidating. Ferguson (2011) explores some of the very difficult issues that can make it hard to undertake home visits and even harder to focus on what is happening within the home. It may be easier to force ourselves to visit when there are definite questions to be asked, rather than when we have no agenda other than to experience what being at home means for a young child, in a home where we are not welcome visitors.

It is important to acknowledge the very real concerns that may make it difficult, if not impossible, to observe within the home environment, to talk about these with your manager and ensure that a way forward is found that guarantees your safety and enables you to find other places to observe and other ways of spending time with the child. It is also important to think about what your feelings of fear may (or may not) tell you about what it is like to live in that home, possibly feeling all the time what you feel when you visit.

We need to ask ourselves:

* Where does the fear comes from (something we are observing/sensing in this situation, or something within us – from our own past experience)?

* Where does it belong (in this flat, something feels very wrong, or does someone in this family remind us of someone else we have known who was intimidating)?

* What does it mean, in terms of the children living with this and for any other members of the household?

COMMENT

When I worked in an area office where, tragically, a colleague had been murdered, I initially felt terrified of undertaking home visits in the road where she was killed, although this was not a neighbourhood where there were any difficulties, and I felt like this regardless of whether there were any risks associated with the family I was visiting. In this example, the fear came from my own experience, knowing that my colleague had not been aware of the risk to which she was exposed and then inappropriately projecting my fears into other situations, where they did not belong.

While this may seem a rather extreme example to draw on, as thankfully such tragedies are rare, it is important to acknowledge that fear is often present, particularly in relation to home visits, and it can block our ability to see, to observe and to think.

What do social workers mean by 'observation'?

Before looking at examples of the use of observation by practitioners, it is perhaps helpful to note that all of the practitioners whom I interviewed shared a broadly holistic, experiential approach to undertaking observations, informed by training at qualifying and/or postqualifying levels. However, their practice also varied in significant ways. For some it was a planned, conscious process, with minimal activity and a careful focus on the minutiae of the situation.

> It's about watching rather than reacting ... about believing that there are reasons behind what the child is doing, but you have to **watch very closely** to see that. Often they are reacting to something. I've realised how important small things are to children.

> It's about being quiet and watching.

> Seeing, being, absorbing, you need to centre yourself ... getting a sense of what is happening.

> Seeing in a pure sense, the behaviour and interaction of the child/parent. You have to switch everything else off (and not think about what the solution might be).

Others talked about being receptive, including noticing information received through their senses and recognising the feelings that particular situations evoked in them.

> *It might make you feel a particular way – happy, uncomfortable, anxious.*

> *It includes what you are taking in from what is going on around you.*

> *Sometimes we have gut feelings that something does not fit, for example hearing a lot of shouting when approaching a flat, but when you knock and do the visit, there is a sense of a happy façade that does not fit with what you have just heard.*

> *On reflection, smell is also very important, especially in neglect cases. I was probably more aware of using my senses when I was newly qualified – perhaps around a worry that I was not seeing what I expected. I would record my thinking. I would have to describe what I had seen that made me think that something was wrong. I might then ask someone to come out with me.*

For others, observing was important, but was not an explicit focus of their work.

> *I don't think about observation consciously, but it underpins all my practice.*

> *Observation was always part of the work I did, I did it without knowing I was doing it. I mostly did it alongside undertaking an assessment and asking questions.*

> *I think we often observe without consciously thinking about it: we probably do it more than we realise.*

> *As a part of a child protection visit I just sit and see what's going on.*

> *I observe all the time, but it would be rare for me to go out just to observe. I like to make it feel as relaxed as possible and develop a relationship, often through play with children. But, if there was a particular worry, eg that a parent did not know how to play, I might arrange to observe.*

And for others, their workloads and the practice setting limited the opportunities.

> *It's not really possible to do it separately because of time constraints, although in the context of a visit, I may just sit and watch for a while.*

Activity

In your practice, what might be the advantages of planning a visit to a child or family, where you have explained that your main purpose is to observe them?

What are the disadvantages?

COMMENT

Your thoughts on the advantages and disadvantages may include issues related to the opportunity to really focus on the child, family and setting, weighed against time, not getting answers to particular questions and the awkwardness of being an observer and explaining what you plan to do.

Another important issue that you may have considered is transparency. How do we ensure that families are partners in the process of assessment?

Examples of the use of observation

Setting it up

While Chapter 3 explored the main issues that need to be considered when setting up observations, including assent and consent, in this chapter the focus is on how this may work in practice. The following examples are drawn from practice in situations where there are or have been child protection concerns.

> I regularly say to parents I want to come and observe you with the children – let's just see what happens in your house when the children come home. I can learn about the routines in their house. I reassure them that it's just a glimpse and recognise that it will be different with me there. I explain that it's not a normal visit, I am just going to watch – to the parents and children. Sometimes it is very hard as inevitably children want to interact so I try to minimise what I do. Usually I find it takes 5–10 minutes before people start to be less aware of me. In an hour's observation I probably catch a good 20–25 minutes of what's going on in the home.

> Usually I book observations as part of an assessment.

> If a parent has said they are too busy for me to visit, I might say don't worry that's fine, carry on with whatever you are doing and I will just follow you around.

> I explain to parents, but my observations are usually part of an assessment or child protection plan, so consent is not generally an issue that is separately explored, as they accept observation as part of the process.

In these examples the social workers have explained in various ways that they will be observing what happens and consent has largely been assumed as part of the non-negotiable involvement of a social worker. However, there was general agreement that a different approach to consent should be taken with children at home and at school, as illustrated by this comment:

> I would always ask the child if they felt okay about seeing me at school because it can feel weird.

In a different context, a health professional used the following approach, also useful in residential or day-care settings.

> *You can make opportunities to observe by asking about how they play or what they do … being quiet and watching, you can pick up on their interactions. It can be for just a few minutes.*

> *It's a time when you are fortunate to sit with a family, but don't contribute, **watching the tiny little things** – a mother pulling back – seeing the dance between them … being silent … being quiet.*

Level of participation

While for some, careful planning in relation to the level of participation was important, others stressed a more flexible, pragmatic approach.

> *Sometimes I might observe in a nursery; whether I also engage or not depends on the situation.*

The need at times to respond to something in the moment is a challenge for all observers and is often a central preoccupation in seminar discussion groups. Potentially it distracts from the complete focus on those we are observing as we switch our attention to thinking about our response and our own actions. Moreover, our intervention may change what is happening: the bored child is no longer bored if we read them a story! Fagan (2014: 95) suggests that the concept of 'sway' may be helpful for those observing children. She explains that the observer needs to imagine how they are seen by the child and to find

> *a place that is neither so neutral that it risks being seen as dismissive by the child, nor so involved that it leads to a confusion of roles and boundaries, in relation both to the young child and their parents.*

> (Fagan 2014: 80)

This suggests that a slight change in emphasis can be appropriate in some situations, but not a complete change of role. It always important to think about why we feel a need to adopt a more active role and to consider what the impact of this may be. Engaging in action can be a way of avoiding or changing an otherwise unbearable situation.

How practitioners used observations

Observation can arguably provide the only way of beginning to understand the experience of babies and very young children who cannot otherwise tell us about what is happening and how it feels from their point of view. Similarly, the value of observing children who have little or no language was stressed by some. This health professional described how her training in observation shaped her practice. For her it meant

> *being quiet and watching, taking the moments that you get in every interaction and capturing them. I use observation alongside assessment and also as a therapeutic tool … I notice where parents put their babies.*

In assessments, her careful, very detailed observations were able to inform her understanding.

> It is really important in situations where you are worried to see if the visual impact is the same as what you are being told, for example, flinching or drawing away. It could be by the mother, or the baby or both. If I observe this I will then ask about it, did you notice that you pulled back when ...

> In another situation I was weighing an 8-week-old baby, who just stared at the ceiling, not making eye contact with me or his mother. It made me feel anxious and made me question what was happening for the baby. When he was not with his mother, he was able to make eye contact with the social worker.

Primarily social workers talked about using observations to inform and supplement information gathered for assessments.

> In child protection it's important to evidence how you see the child: I can include extracts from my observations in court reports.

> I use observation in all assessments. Parents may tell you about how a child behaves. If you then go and observe it may be quite different and you can see how the parent responds. For example, when children come home from school you might see one child being ignored, the forgotten child in the household.

> In one situation a young child put his hands over his ears and ran to his mum when he heard loud noises. We were then able to ask his mum about why this was. She explained that he was worried it would be the police, who often came to the house to search for drugs.

Observing in different settings

The importance of observing children on a number of occasions and in different contexts was stressed by several practitioners, in order to minimise the possibility of things being 'set up' to impress them, as well as to observe how children were with different carers and in different situations.

> I observed children in their home context, at different times of day, with each parent and at school or nursery.

> I observed very aggressive behaviour by a young child when he was at home. He was hitting out, stamping and throwing toys, but he was completely different at nursery.

Movement

Ferguson (2011) reminds us that much can be learned from observing movement. How, where and when children move may tell us about their experience. Stillness, watchfulness and avoidance may also be revealing, as in the following examples.

The child ran into the room, then veered off when he saw his mother, hitting the table and falling to the floor. He seemed unsure of how she would respond, so he had quickly changed direction to avoid running into her.

In another example, where a plan had been agreed to address concerns about neglect, the social worker had agreed with the mother that she would do unannounced visits to observe how things were going. The little boy was 22 months old.

When I arrived mum's eyes were slightly puffy and she was wearing her pyjamas. Jason was wearing a T shirt and a nappy. I sat down on the floor and then noticed that his skin seemed very pale, almost translucent and his nose was running. As mum moved around and went into the kitchen he stayed still, watching her until she was out of sight. His nose was streaming. When she came back in with a coffee for both of us he looked at her with very wide eyes, but remained well away from his mum, quiet and still as I chatted with her.

Looking at him made me think of the descriptions of frozen watchfulness that I had read about.

Similarly, as we were reminded in Chapter 2, four-year-old Daniel Pelka trailed behind his mother when collected from school. His movements might not have been concerning with an older child, but were noticed at the time by the teaching assistant and provided another window into his relationship with his mother.

Mealtimes

Mealtimes can also be particularly revealing for observers, although ensuring that this is accomplished with minimal discomfort for those observed requires careful negotiation. One social worker described a situation with a six-month-old baby where there were concerns about parenting skills.

I observed a mealtime. The mother was rushing and giving the baby very large mouthfuls, not picking up on the cues from the baby who was unable to manage the amount of food. He would pull back and close his mouth, but as soon as it was less tightly shut, she still tried to get the spoon in.

And in another situation with a six-year-old, the social worker

observed a child refusing to eat, getting upset. Some of the other children were allowed to go to the fridge and eat whatever they wanted. The parent was not aware that she was very inconsistent in her approach and so the child felt that they could easily get away with not doing as they were told. I could see there were no clear boundaries.

Using observation within an interview

The following example illustrates the social worker holding an observational stance as a participant observer, while talking with the mother.

When I was talking to a parent I saw the child hurt his hand. He held it and was looking at it, but then approached me to seek comfort rather than his mother. Later during the assessment process I was able to ask his mother what she thought about this and why her son might have done this.

Others commented on the value of using observations of children alongside what was being presented, or what a child or parent was telling them.

In a case where a little boy wanted to be with his father, his behaviour and visible distress when taken back to his mother confirmed what he was also telling me ... and with another child the behaviour that I observed did not fit with what she was saying.

When you are observing contact you look at the child and think about whether their behaviour fits with what they are telling you.

In another case I noticed on one occasion that the bedroom door was closed, whereas it was normally open: it was made clear to me that I could not look inside. The mother's non-verbal communication was also awkward and I sensed there was something not right. It subsequently transpired that her boyfriend was in the bedroom.

Observation was also used to help understand the actual parenting that was being displayed, as opposed to what the mother said she did.

I observed a mother ignoring her daughter – she is always on the phone and texting when I visit, with the child coming to me for attention and climbing on to my lap.

These examples demonstrate the value of thinking about the connections, or indeed the disconnections, between what is said and what is observed.

Observing young people

Finding ways of engaging with young people can be challenging. Activities can be helpful, as can taking the pressure off by saying:

We don't need to talk, I'd just like to spend some time with you, getting to know how things are for you/how you spend your day.

This frees both the young person and the social worker from the awkwardness of contrived conversations and leaves space for an attuned attentiveness.

In the following two examples the social worker has gained important insights into the young person's experience by observing in the context of their family.

I was working with a young person where certain safeguards needed to be put in place to manage any risk around potential sexually abusive behaviour towards other children. The parents wanted to tell their daughter about what needed to happen. I was there to support and explain, but I was also able to observe. I observed the young person becoming more and more upset. She was close to tears, but her parents did not see, or did not respond, to the cues from their daughter and appeared not to see the impact of their criticism on her.

I had an uneasy feeling. I asked a colleague to do a visit. We then realised that some small details of what we saw were at odds with the parenting behaviours that we would normally see – Dad carefully combing out his 12-year-old daughter's hair, with an expression that was hard to place, and adjusting her clothing. This led us to talk to the children and about the care provided by Dad, which revealed very serious issues.

Observing signs of domestic abuse

Experience within local domestic abuse services as well as from a range of research studies (Humphreys 1999; McGee 2000; Abrahams 2010) indicates that women experiencing domestic abuse often hide this from social workers, fearful of the consequences of disclosure. For social workers it may be hard to find effective ways of beginning the conversation and providing support (Radford and Hester 2006). One way of approaching this is to comment on what has been observed, which can then provide a basis for sensitive exploration of the impact of what is happening to the woman herself, as in the following examples.

I noticed that you looked startled and jumped when the door banged – but it was just the wind. I wondered what made you feel like that? … I was wondering if you were worried about Sam (her partner) coming home?

I noticed bruising on her, grab marks. She would never talk about it or admit that there was domestic violence, although subsequently when she was in a different relationship she did talk about it.

Family placement work

The particular value of using observation to understand sibling relationships in order to make decisions about future placements, together, in groups or separately was highlighted in the following examples.

With a family I already knew quite well, I observed them for an extended period in one day, so that I could see how the children interacted and how the parents coped. I just sat on the sofa and moved around with them.

I try to go at important times of day so that I can see interactions, after school, tea time, bed time, etc. It is always important to recognise that my presence has an impact on the situation and may change what is happening.

I use information from observation to correlate or contrast with information from other sources (people's opinions). But, need to be careful, a one-off observation has little validity without context.

This social worker, as in the earlier example, considered that over time the 'observer effect' diminished, hence she found extended observations particularly useful.

Using observation in interventions

In addition to the central role of observation in assessment, observation can also be used in the context of intervention in many different ways. Blessing and Block (2014: 211) describe the '*unanticipated therapeutic impact*' that observation may have. Simply being present and not making demands when we are working with parents can be very helpful, providing the observed with a sense that the observer has seen life from their perspective and has some understanding of what they are going through, as illustrated in the following example.

> *Parents often find it really helpful to* **have an outside pair of eyes** *who can say how it seems to them and make suggestions. They say to me, you've seen how he behaved.*

> *It's really important not to be judgemental. I try to feed back on what I have seen and pick up on the strengths. I don't see any mileage in observation unless you can feed it back to the family. In every family there are strengths and safely factors.*

> *I think observation is particularly helpful with boundary setting in families where it is chaotic. You might observe a mealtime and see one child being treated very differently – allowed to sit and eat on the floor, where the others are eating at the table, or one child goes to the fridge and chooses what they want, but is not noticed. The focus may be on the other children who mum is listening and responding to, but she is unaware of the differences in the way she is responding to the children. So, I feed back what I observe and that provides the basis for thinking about how things may need to change.*

In these examples the social worker has maintained an observational stance, but later explores what she has observed with the families, providing a supportive space for them to reflect on what is happening.

Noticing and reinforcing positive behaviours

> *Mum was actually very playful, but lacked confidence and was asking how she should play with her baby. I observed the things that the baby was responding to and fed that back to her, 'Oh, she's really responding, did you notice that she's listening to you, she reached out to try to pat you.' The mum was very pleased and it helped her to realise that her baby was a little person.*

In provider settings there can be many opportunities to observe, but the following observation illustrates the value of observing without any agenda, so that we are open to becoming aware of things that we were not necessarily looking for.

> *I observed the mothers becoming engrossed in play (craft activities). They wanted to play with us and would carry on with the activity long after the children had lost*

interest and wandered off. I felt that they needed nurturing and wanted to play. They were often very pleased with what they had done.

In this situation the observer was able to provide a safe environment where the mothers were briefly free from their normal responsibilities and were able to take pleasure in expressing themselves through creative play. The observer's quiet acceptance legitimised their engagement in play as something worthwhile.

Recording

As we saw in Chapter 3, recording presents many challenges for observers and it is rarely a favourite task for any practitioner. However, if the finer details of what is observed are to be recalled, it is essential that recording is a priority, as the details and the feelings fade from our memories very rapidly. The following examples reflect the ways in which practitioners approached the task.

I do take notes at the same time if I am noting facts, but not if I am sitting with a child.

The following comment reflects the recognition that taking notes when observing can be distracting, both for the observer and the observed, especially for children and young people.

I usually record afterwards, or at the end of the visit, with the child. It distracts me from listening and watching and it's not a natural environment if you are writing. Children can feel as if they are being tested.

With a child I may then agree with them what notes I will record and may include a verbatim section of what they have said.

In these examples practitioners have found ways of ensuring that they undertake some recording either at the end of the observation or very soon afterwards. However, it may be very difficult to reflect and think about any feelings or more nebulous perceptions until we are in a quiet space on our own, but the pressures of time can make this difficult.

Sometimes I include feelings, but time is an issue when recording.

I have found that making brief notes in the car, or on the bus, after an observation can be helpful. Others have used mobile phones to record immediate observations, which can then be used as an *aide-mémoire* when writing up the observation more fully, using the headings suggested in Chapter 3.

One of the issues often raised by practitioners on post-qualifying courses is the concern about recording things that those they are observing may not agree with, or may be unaware of. Another issue raised was the tension between being descriptive and detailed, as they are encouraged to be more analytical.

COMMENT

It is always important to share such concerns in supervision, as they are likely to reflect issues that need deeper consideration. The suggestions for recording in the previous chapter may help to ensure that what you record is appropriately detailed and provides a basis for reflective analysis.

Making sense of observations

Observers may need to be prepared for their colleagues to hold quite different views to their own about what has been observed, as in the following example:

> On one occasion I went into a group with other professionals, mothers and babies. The baby fell forward, bumped her nose and cried. The mother laughed: I saw a mismatch in the response to the baby, but this was dismissed by the other professionals.

Activity

How might you react in this situation? Why might the respective professionals hold different views about whether this was funny, or whether there was something to be concerned about in this situation?

COMMENT

Reasons for these varied reactions may include some of the issues discussed earlier in this chapter, such as identity, professional backgrounds, training and experience as observers. Some may have noticed the baby falling, but not observed the mother's response to the baby. Some may have been focused on the interaction and participation in the group, whereas the observer seems to have been able to focus on what the experience of falling and his mother's response meant for the baby.

The importance of being able to talk about what has been observed and the feelings that this has evoked cannot be overstated. Without this, there is a serious risk that we will be unable to make sense of what we are seeing. In difficult and distressing situations, we may be disturbed or overwhelmed in ways that we are barely conscious of, as illustrated in Chapter 1. Good supervision therefore has a central role in ensuring safe and effective practice. Social workers saw this as the ideal place to talk about anything that did not feel right.

However, it is unfortunately necessary to acknowledge that this is not always possible or available, so it is useful to think about additional ways of processing what has been observed. Some people find it is helpful to write about they are feeling, as the process of writing can bring clarity to our thinking. Others found talking to experienced colleagues very helpful. Another approach is to develop your own structured approaches to reflection, as in the following examples.

I ask myself, what does what I have observed mean in terms of the child, and in terms of me. I am very aware of how that affects my thinking.

I use a rigorous process of self-questioning:

- *Is this what I saw?*
- *Is this what I think I saw?*

I ask myself, what have I seen and does that match what I am hearing?

Activity

In your practice setting, how can you ensure that you have a reflective space to process what you are observing?

COMMENT

While some organisational contexts facilitate this process, others do not. As a professional social worker it is important to recognise that this is an essential part of your practice and to take responsibility for this process. You may want to develop a set of questions that you could use to help your reflection, and these could also be explored in supervision. Refer back to Chapter 3 for the questions on reflecting on your observation and consider how you might adapt these for your practice.

Limitations: the observer effect

Concerns that naturalistic observation cannot attain the levels of objectivity required for the behavioural sciences are well established (Denzin 2005; Hammersley 1992; Robson 2011). The extent to which people may consciously and/or unconsciously change their behaviour in the presence of an observer will be affected by what they hope to achieve from manipulating their behaviour. It is therefore always important to consider how and in what ways your presence may be altering what is happening. In practice the ability to sustain such changed behaviour seems to diminish over time and it is particularly difficult for young children to do this without it appearing unnatural.

Difficulties may also arise from within the observer. What we are bringing, perhaps in terms of our previous personal or professional experience, or from our desperate hope that our worst fears have been allayed, which may then lead us to the wrong conclusion.

*Gut instinct can be really wrong. You always need to ask **what is it that is making me think that?** Insecure children cry out for the happy moments, so just because you observe a child being smiley and going to their parents for a hug, you can think all is well, and then the child can get lost, because you are wrong.*

Context is really important, you cannot rely on a single observation.

The cautionary note sounded by these practitioners reflects concerns echoed by many others in my discussions with them, as well as in Serious Case Reviews such as those into the deaths of Kimberley Carlile (London Borough of Greenwich 1987) and Victoria Climbié (Laming 2003). There is a risk that we may want to be reassured that all is well and therefore cling to a brief observation of something which is perhaps untypical, or may have been stage-managed to deliberately mislead professionals. Or we may minimise the importance of something that we have observed, if we are falsely reassured by an explanation given to us that is also designed to mislead us.

While there are no easy answers and there will continue to be occasions when we are unable to see and understand what is happening in a family, these difficulties can perhaps best be addressed by a systematic approach to observation, seeing children over a period of time and, where appropriate, in different settings and with different carers. Inadequate resources and time pressures may mean that this is difficult to achieve, in which case it needs to be acknowledged that the likelihood of properly understanding what it is like to be the child in the family is significantly diminished.

Top tips for observers

Trevithick (2012) has developed a very helpful list of common errors when observing (Figure 4.1).

---

1. Failing to see the significance of what we are observing due to …

2. Failing to link our observations to what is known about the behaviour, situation or individual in question.

3. Being unaware of our assumptions and preconceptions.

4. Failing to give adequate importance to factors that may give rise to certain behaviour, reactions or events.

5. Being imprecise or woolly in our account of the behaviour or events we observe.

6. Generalising behaviour in ways that may not be accurate, for example, what occurs at one time, in one setting may not occur in other settings, or at other times.

7. Being too hasty in our need to draw conclusions from our observations.

8. Assuming that the agreement of others implies accuracy and valid inferences have been formulated (groupthink).

Figure 4.1 Common errors when observing (Trevithick 2012: 169–70)

The following list draws on Trevithick's work and the points made previously in this book providing 'dos' rather than 'don'ts':

•   Be aware of the impact of our own identity, assumptions and preconceptions.

•   Recognise the significance of what we observe and be prepared to examine what this means.

•   Link observations to what is already known about the behaviour, situation or individual in question. If it does not seem to fit, explore why.

- Recognise the importance of factors that may give rise to certain behaviour, reactions or events.

- Be precise, detailed and specific in our accounts of what we observe.

- Recognise that what occurs at one time, in one setting, may not be occurring in other settings, or at other times, or when we are not present.

- Always adopt a systematic approach to observation and seek to triangulate what we have learned from observing (see Chapter 3).

- Stay with uncertainty and maintain openness to new possibilities as new information emerges and situations change.

- If what we have observed leads to us to feel uncomfortable or concerned when others are not, we need to seek further evidence before we let go of our view.

Conclusion

The examples above show the wide range of ways in which observations may enrich practice, in relation to both assessment and intervention. Where practitioners feel confident and are able to use observation as part of a transparent, planned dimension of their practice it has the greatest potential to shine light on the realities of lived experience, for both the observer and the observed. As one practitioner said:

> It's a wonderful tool in our hectic world. Practitioners should all have that opportunity.

While observation is a wonderful tool, providing space to listen to what children want to tell us and checking out their views about what has been observed is also essential, with any child who is able to do so.

Taking it further

Bridge, G and Miles, G (1996) *On the Outside Looking In*. London: Central Council for Education and Training in Social Work.

Flemming, S (2004) The Contribution of Psychoanalytical Observation to Child Protection Assessments. *Journal of Social Work Practice*, 18(2): 223–8.

International Journal of Infant Observation and Its Applications. London: Routledge, www.tandfonline.com/toc/riob20/current#.VeciWCVVikp.

Le Riche, P and Tanner, K (1998) *Observation and Its Application to Social Work*. London: Jessica Kingsley.

Unwin, P and Hogg, R (2012) *Effective Social Work with Children and Families: A Skills Handbook*. London: Sage.

Urwin, C and Sternberg, J (eds) (2012) *Infant Observation and Research: Emotional Processes in Everyday Lives*. London: Routledge.

References

Abrahams, H (2010) *Rebuilding Lives after Domestic Violence.* London: Jessica Kingsley.

Blessing, D and Block, K (2014) Sewing on a Shadow: Acquiring Dimensionality in a Participant Observation, in Simonetta, M, Adamo, G and Rustin, M (eds) *Young Child Observation: A Development in the Method of Infant Observation.* London: Karnac.

Denzin, N and Lincoln, Y (eds) (2005) *The Sage Handbook of Qualitative Research*, 3rd edn. Thousand Oaks, CA: Sage.

Fagan, M (2014) The Young Child Observation Seminar: New Steps in Developing the Observer Role, in Simonetta, M, Adamo, G and Rustin, M (eds) *Young Child Observation: A Development in the Method of Infant Observation.* London: Karnac.

Ferguson, H (2011) *Child Protection Practice.* Basingstoke: Palgrave Macmillan.

Hammersley, M (1992) *What's Wrong with Ethnography?* London: Sage.

Humphreys, C (1999) Avoidance and Confrontation: The Practice of Social Workers in Relation to Domestic Violence and Child Abuse. *Journal of Child and Family Social Work,* 4(1): 77–87.

Laming, Lord (2003) *The Victoria Climbié Inquiry*, CM 5730. London: The Stationery Office, www.gov.uk/government/uploads/system/uploads/attachment_data/file/273183/5730.pdf (accessed 22 September 2015).

Lawler, S (2014) *Identity,* 2nd edn. Cambridge: Polity Press.

Le Riche, P and Tanner, K (1998) *Observation and Its Application to Social Work.* London: Jessica Kingsley.

London Borough of Greenwich (1987) *A Child in Mind: The Report of the Commission of Inquiry into the Circumstances Surrounding the Death of Kimberley Carlile.* London Borough of Greenwich.

McGee, C (2000) Children's and Mothers' Experiences of Support and Protection Following Domestic Violence, in Hanmer, J and Itzin, C (eds) *Home Truths about Domestic Violence: Feminist Influences on Policy and Practice. A Reader.* London: Routledge.

Mullaly, B (2010) *Challenging Oppression and Confronting Privilege,* 2nd edn. Ontario: Oxford University Press.

Radford, L and Hester, M (2006) *Mothering through Domestic Violence.* London: Jessica Kingsley.

Robson, C (2011) *Real World Research*, 3rd edn. Oxford: Wiley-Blackwell.

Simonetta, M, Adamo, G and Rustin, M (eds) (2014) *Young Child Observation: A Development in the Method of Infant Observation.* London: Karnac.

Trevithick, P (2012) *Social Work Skills and Knowledge*, 3rd edn. Maidenhead: Open University Press.

5 Making sense of what we observe: theory helps!

Objectives

This chapter will:

- enable you to reflect on the process of forming and exercising judgement;

- demonstrate the value of theory and research in understanding children's experiences;

- highlight relevant theoretical concepts and research;

- provide examples that illustrate the way in which theory can increase our understanding of practice issues.

Introduction

In the previous chapters the importance of staying in the present and remaining with uncertainty has been emphasised. As we have seen, the process of observation entails being receptive, open and self-aware, so that we are attuned to the fine detail of the experience of those whom we are observing. The observer is also required to notice their own affective responses to what they have observed, paying attention to them and considering how they contribute to their understanding of the person whom they are observing. This process yields a mass of information of different types which can be overwhelming. Much, if not all, of the information is highly subjective. As observers collect information from a range of sources, some of it will conflict and result in uncertainty, so it is necessary to have ways of sifting and analysing it that go beyond the observer's own personal experience and frame of reference.

Findings from research and theoretical concepts can provide observers with information and frameworks to help them to make sense of their experience and of the information that has been gathered; a vital step before forming a view about what it means. Recognising that some readers may be unsure about their ability to draw on theoretical concepts to inform their practice, the process will be illustrated with reference to the case study of Dara.

The chapter draws on an eclectic range of material, reflecting the wide knowledge base that social work is informed by. It will not attempt to provide a detailed explanation of each of the theoretical concepts, but will attempt to provide sufficient information to illustrate how it may be used to enable practitioners to reflect on their experience as observers and to think about the child's experience, as well as that of her carers. The content of this chapter has deliberately been placed at the end of the book to reflect the need to observe first and then to reflect and make sense of the observation with reference to theory, rather than to place theory first and then attempt to fit the observation to a theory.

The following will be considered:

- the process of exercising judgement;

- child development checklists;

- attachment theory;

- containment;

- loss and separation;

- transference and counter transference;

- the use of research findings.

Further reading will be suggested to enable readers to explore in more depth any research or theoretical concepts that they wish to learn more about.

Perception and the exercise of judgement

As with perception and interpretation, judgement happens automatically and at an unconscious level, below the surface of our awareness. Just as Tanner and Le Riche (1998) refer to observation as 'rather like breathing', so Camus (1956) suggests that 'to breathe is to judge' (quoted in Thiele 2006: 2). While until this point in the book the importance of staying open to uncertainty has been emphasised, the process of judging at an unconscious level will already be happening. According to the neuroscientist V. S. Ramachandran, every act of perception involves an act of judgement by the brain (Thiele 2006: 3). The essential next step is to explore these unconscious judgements and evaluate their meaning as part of the process of evaluation and consciously exercising judgement: an essential prerequisite for planning future actions.

Over the millennia philosophers have sought to understand and identify the characteristics of wisdom and judgement, but it was not until the second half of the twentieth century that neuroscientists and cognitive psychologists were able to see the workings of the brain and so better understand the interplay of conscious and unconscious processes that operate when judgement is being exercised. Thiele (2006) explains that:

> Human judgement is a hybrid faculty. Blending rational, perceptual, and affective capacities, operating at the conscious level and below the threshold of awareness, taking heed of hard facts as well as narrative coherence, the human judge manages to forge meaningful patterns from a blooming, buzzing world.

> (Thiele 2006: ix)

While for social workers the world may not always feel as if it is blooming, the important point here is the confirmation that conscious rational thought and unconscious intuitive thought operate alongside each other; that *'good judgement demands whole-brain learning'* (Thiele 2006: 162). Intuitive thinking and rational analysis are not, as was once thought, polar opposites, but are most effective when both are used together, complementing each other.

Observations of children and families that we are working with may include perceptions that we are unconscious of, which may provide us with intuitive (unconscious) understandings of what is happening. However, while these may provide a useful starting point, Thiele explains that there are important caveats to be aware of in relation to intuition:

> Intuition tends to be automatic (experienced passively), rapid, effortless, holistic (pattern orientated) and associational .... grasping reality in concrete images and metaphors, [intuition] is self-evidently valid and is prone to stereotyping. Intuition is immediately compelling and resistant to change.
>
> (Thiele 2006: 135)

A further difficulty when using information gained through our senses is that we are frequently working with *feelings*, which within contemporary Western society are often juxtaposed with *reason* and *rationality* and considered to be unreliable, and so they are often set aside, or even dismissed (Butler 2007). However, as we think about how we interpret what has been observed, it is perhaps more helpful to think about feelings having a significant role in determining *meaning*, adding colour and texture to a picture that is otherwise monochrome. Feelings and intuition may provide important insights, but need to be contextualized and used together with rational thought, as part of the story, not the only story.

Another helpful contribution to the understanding of judgement in social work comes from the work of Hammond (2007), who has applied developments in cognitive psychology to the analysis of social and political dilemmas facing decision-makers who are surrounded by uncertainty. He introduces the term *multiple fallible indicators* to refer to the myriad, varied forms of information that people absorb and collect in all sorts of different ways, from hard empirical facts to sensory perceptions that have been absorbed unconsciously. The inclusion of the word *fallible* is helpful in drawing attention to the unreliability of any single piece of information, or indeed observation. Similarly the term *indicator* reminds us that a piece of information may point to something being the case, but does not necessarily establish something as a fact. Some of the indicators may be in conflict with others, so generating great uncertainty, both in relation to the reliability of the information collected (what is really happening) and on a personal subjective level (can I do this, I feel confused, did I really see that ...?). Some of the indicators that we draw on may describe surface aspects of a person that we can see (cleanliness, dress, language), but we often use them to infer depth characteristics such as trustworthiness, honesty and parenting capacity (Hammond 2007: 128).

Activity

Read the following extract from the case study about Dara and her mother. Imagine that you have been allocated to this case. List the fallible indicators: some will be from the referral and some from the observations.

Notice where surface characteristics may be used to infer depth characteristics.

Case Study: Dara

Dara is a three-year-old girl. She has attended a nursery for the last six months for three days a week while her mother is out at work. Children's Social Care Safeguarding Team has received a further domestic abuse notification from the police. The notification states that Maria Garcia, Dara's mother, was unwilling to press charges and that her partner had gone out when they arrived. Maria had a cut above her left eye which she claimed had happened when she was pushed and then fell against the door. Neighbours told the police that there was often shouting and screaming and that the little girl cried a lot. On a visit following up these concerns, you observe that:

> When Maria opened the door Dara was clinging to her leg. In order to move from the door Maria firmly unwrapped Dara's arms and pulled her up saying, 'Let go Dara, let the lady in.' Dara looked up at her mum, who held out her hand as they exchanged a brief smile. I noticed that Dara was very slightly built, an attractive little girl with dark, curly hair and big brown eyes. She was wearing a clean red track suit that seemed rather big for her.

> She then trotted beside her mother, still holding her hand tightly, as we went into the living room. I thought Maria moved a little stiffly, choosing a chair in the far corner, rather than sitting in the low chair next to the one that she showed me to. The room was quite bare, but clean and very tidy. Dara climbed quickly on to her mother's lap as soon as they were sitting, partially obscuring Maria's face from my line of view. Maria pushed her off with a sigh and said 'It's okay Dara, go and play.' Dara looked at me throughout this exchange, and when I smiled at her and said 'Hello', she looked away. It gave me a sense of uncertainty and made me feel unsure about how to respond to her.

> She then sat by her mother's feet and stayed quite still throughout my visit as I tried to talk with Maria. There were some dolls and toys stacked neatly in the corner, but she did not show any interest in them.

> Maria seemed very reluctant to engage with me and I was unsure how much this was due to Dara's presence, and how much because she wanted to deny that there were any problems.

As a follow-up to the visit, it was agreed with Dara and Maria that you could visit the nursery so you could find out how Dara was when she was at nursery. You made the following observation:

> When I arrived I noticed she was wandering around the room, looking around with her eyes wide open. She seemed unable to settle. I found myself feeling anxious, but I wasn't sure why. She picked up some pretend food and put it in her mouth, then quickly put it down again when another boy approached her. She ran outside and ran about in the corridor until a member of staff (her keyworker?) asked her to stay in one of the rooms. The member of staff guided her back to the room that she had come from.

She wandered slowly towards the home corner, where there were no other children. She seemed to relax when she went inside the little house, where she could not easily be seen.

She spent some minutes carefully putting pretend food in the play oven, then taking it out and arranging it on a plate. I began to relax as I watched her, at last absorbed in her play.

Suddenly a group of three other girls arrived. The tallest of the three announced loudly that this was not her house and she shouldn't be there. Dara froze and dropped the plate. I seemed to be the only person who had noticed and I suddenly felt very protective, desperately hoping that one of the staff would see what was happening and realise Dara's silent distress: I could see tears coming. However, she did not look for any of the staff, but ran back out into the corridor with her arms wrapped tightly around her chest, as if she was trying to protect herself.

List the *fallible indicators:* some will be from the referral and some from the observations.

Notice where *surface* indicators may be used to infer *depth* characteristics.

COMMENT

You may have found this task difficult, in part because the information is very limited and you may have felt you needed to know more before beginning this task. However, to some extent this mirrors the situation that social workers are often faced with: trying to make judgements on the basis of limited information. The table below gives some examples that your list may have included.

Surface Indicator	Inferred depth characteristic
Neighbours state that Dara cries a lot	She is unhappy/her needs are not being met
Dara clings to her mum and seems reluctant to play	She is anxious
Her clothes seem very loose	She may be underweight/is Mum feeding her appropriately?
She doesn't run around much	Is she anxious about being separated from her mother? Can she trust other adults?
She seemed unsettled in her play at nursery	She is preoccupied: her own needs are unmet
She seemed nervous of the other children	
Maria makes up stories to cover up domestic abuse	She is protecting her partner/she does not trust the police or social workers
Maria moved stiffly and chose not to sit in a low chair	Perhaps the abuse is ongoing and she has other injuries?

Figure 5.1 *Examples of surface indicators and inferred depth characteristics*

Correspondence and coherence

Hammond identifies two approaches to judgement, which he believes are often used unconsciously by people, and which may begin to enable us to understand the way that decisions may be made in Dara's world. These two approaches are *correspondence* and *coherence*.

Correspondence

Here the brain seeks to find further indicators that correspond with the indicators that the person already has, or that establish the truth of the indicators that the observer has noticed. This approach is effective when there are some facts which can establish empirical truths. For example, if the observer had thought that Dara seemed thin and possibly underweight, as she noticed that her clothes seemed loose and baggy, she could liaise with a health visitor to ascertain when Dara last had her height and weight checked. She could find out what was happening in relation to Dara's physical development, which will be discussed further in the next section. This might include liaising with other professionals such as a health visitor to discuss her progress in relation to a centile chart. If one had not previously been completed this would be a good time to work with health professionals to complete one, enabling those concerned to establish a baseline from which to make a decision about whether or not further monitoring was needed.

Coherence

In the absence of any empirical facts, people seek to find a way of establishing coherence or *meaningful patterns* amongst the multiple fallible indicators. The patterns that we consider to be meaningful will be derived from many different sources, including our professional knowledge base, cultural norms and our own personal experience and values. This process is therefore subject to a number of unconscious biases.

Kirkman and Melrose (2014) looked at the judgement and decision-making of social workers receiving child protection referrals, and their findings demonstrate the operation of both the correspondence and coherence strategies identified by Hammond. They identified a tendency to seek out information (indicators) that confirms an existing view as one of a number of cognitive biases that can distort judgement. This 'confirmatory bias' can result in practitioners avoiding seeking out or ignoring information that contradicts their hypothesis. Other sources of bias that they found included (Kirkman and Melrose 2014: 23–6):

- the impact of first impressions;

- the practitioner's emotional reaction;

- the ability to recall similar events and compare them with the present situation;

- groupthink: a reluctance to challenge others and tendency to conform to the majority view;

- avoidance of making hard and emotionally challenging decisions.

In relation to any judgement it is always important to be aware of the operation of biases and to seek indicators from divergent sources, rather than drawing on the same sources which may simply confirm the existing thinking.

The next part of the chapter will explore some relevant tools and theoretical concepts that can provide frameworks for establishing coherence.

Child development checklists

While the concept of child development as an age-related linear process was problematised in the first chapter, in relation to children's competence and right to participate, it can nevertheless be a valuable concept when attempting to understand children's well-being. Observers may notice many aspects of a child's development, but without a frame of reference it may be hard to understand the significance of what has been observed.

Child development checklists are compiled from data gathered by researchers testing, measuring, observing and collating information about children's developmental progress. Sometimes this includes using particular tests, for example, to see at what age most children can complete a particular task. These can provide a baseline for thinking about many aspects of development, including height and weight, speech and language development, social behaviour, play and self-care skills. While this type of data may provide a reasonable starting point, as was shown in the first chapter, it will necessarily be constrained by the cultural context in which it was gathered.

The value of such tools is recognised by the inclusion of Mary Sheridan's 'Chart illustrating the developmental progress of infants and young children' in the Department of Health's *Assessing Children in Need and their Families: Practice Guidance* (DoH 2000: 23–8). This can be used in conjunction with the Royal College of Paediatrics and Child Health growth charts (2009) as a starting point for reflecting on what has been observed.

It is, however, always important to question the relevance of any framework to the individual child as there are very significant variations in the pace of children's development. Harris (2008, pp 5–6) uses the analogy of a ball rolling down through a valley. The nature of the ball (whether it is entirely smooth, its weight, etc.), the steepness of the incline and so on will determine the speed that the ball travels at. The course is constrained by the landscape, but it will still reach the valley floor. Similarly, children's development is affected by a wide range of factors, and whether these are seen as positive is, in part at least, culturally determined. A good example of the impact of context can be seen in relation to views about the age at which bladder and bowel control may be achieved. The availability of disposable nappies has been accompanied by many young children in the United Kingdom wearing nappies for much longer than they did in the 1950s. By contrast, in northern Thailand Shan Burmese babies may not wear nappies at all, but are simply changed frequently and held out to urinate and defecate as small babies and so learn to control their bowel and bladder movements at least 18 months earlier than many babies in the UK, where toilet training typically does not begin until well after a child's second birthday.

Hence, within the wider culture, as well as within the individual child and their family, there are many factors which inform people's attitudes and views about the 'right' time and the right way to do things. They are often then defended as the best way, whereas in reality there may be a far broader range of acceptable ways of doing things than is often recognised. These limitations always need to be thought about in relation to the experience and context of the individual child who is being considered, along with any particular needs or issues such as disability that may impact on the child's development.

Our own personal experience will also form a bench mark for judgement.

Activity

Using the weblink to DoH (2000) in the references for this chapter, look at Mary Sheridan's 'Chart illustrating developmental progress'. What have you noticed so far about Dara's developmental progress? What would you like to find out in order to form a view about her development?

COMMENT

The Sheridan chart suggests, amongst other things, that typically a three-year-old might enjoy floor play and joining in with other children. She may talk to herself in long monologues as well as carrying on simple conversations. She might be feeding herself with a fork and spoon. It would be useful therefore to spend more time with Dara in order to gain a better understanding of her play, self-care and language development, as there has so far been little evidence of what she is doing in relation to any of these issues.

It would also be useful to liaise with the health visitor to find out when Dara was last weighed and measured and to discuss this with Maria. Dara's height and weight could be plotted on a growth chart, if this has not already been done, and could be monitored regularly if there are concerns.

Understanding relationships: attachment theory

Attachment theory provides a framework for reflecting on children's relationships with their families and carers. Attachment may be defined as '*an affectionate bond between two individuals that endures through space and time and serves to join them emotionally*' (Klaus and Kennell 1976; cited in Daniel et al 1999, p 16). It may therefore be very helpful when thinking about what has been observed in relation to Dara's emotional well-being and relationship with her parents. A brief summary of aspects relevant to this case study is given below, but readers are strongly encouraged to gain a fuller understanding of attachment theory by reading one of the texts suggested at the end of this chapter.

Attachment theory

The initial notion proposed by Bowlby in the 1950s, that separation from the primary carer (then assumed to be the mother) led to later psychological problems, has proved to be of lasting relevance. He recognised that in order to flourish, infants and young children need to have their needs met in a loving relationship in a consistent enough manner for them to be free to explore their environment safely and without anxiety. While subsequent study and research has challenged the original gendered and culturally specific assumptions, it has also extended our understanding of the original theory, so that it now provides an overarching framework for thinking about close relationships and emotional development (Howe 1999;

Holmes 2001). More recently research (eg Hart 2008) has demonstrated that the development of the brain is affected by early care experiences. Early attachment relationships will therefore have a lasting impact on emotional development and the nature of relationships across the lifespan. Subsequent resilience and the ability to deal with separation and a range of stressful circumstances throughout life are thought to be significantly determined by the nature of early attachment relationships.

Attachment behaviour

Any behaviour designed to get children into a close, protective relationship with their attachment figures whenever they experience anxiety.

(Howe 1999: 14)

Babies and infants will try out a range of approaches to gain attention and ensure that their needs are met. If smiling or crying are not successful then doing something that they know their attachment figures will not want them to do may be the only option! When people are distressed or anxious they tend to use the same type of behaviours to establish closeness and protection throughout their lives. According to Howe:

Whenever people want emotional closeness or experience distress they will either:

* *Behave in a socially appealing manner*
* *Send out distress signals designed to invite attention and concern*
* *Actively approach and seek out others for the things that they believe close relationships can provide.*

(Howe 1999: 15)

Activity

Thinking about going into an unfamiliar social situation yourself, can you identify what type of behaviours you most frequently use?

COMMENT

When discussing this with groups of students, those who use positive strategies tend to find it easy to identify the strategies that they commonly use, such as being very friendly and smiley or targeting someone they know is likely to have something in common with them. They generally find this is successful and experience this as an affirming process. For those who usually send out negative distress signals – whether it is the student who disrupts the seminar by continually playing the fool when they are struggling to understand, or a lover who recognises that they annoy their partner in order to provoke a response – this is not experienced as affirming, although it may reduce the anxiety that provoked the behaviour.

Case study (continued): Dara and her father

Fifteen months later and Dara has just turned four years old. She is in her first term at school. The school have contacted the duty team in Children's Services. They are concerned that Dara's attendance has been very erratic and she seems to have more bumps and bruises than they would expect. In the playground she is a quiet, unadventurous child, so it is hard to understand how this is happening. She says she just falls over a lot. Given what is already known about the family, you are asked to visit.

> It takes a long time before the door is answered by a man whom I have not met before, but later discover is Jason, Maria's partner and Dara's father. During my discussion with him I ask where Dara is. He then gets up and shouts 'Come here you daft git, you know I didn't mean it!' He sounded very irritated to me. I wondered how Dara was feeling.
>
> There was no response so Jason went out of the room and returned a few minutes later with Dara, firmly guiding (pushing?) her into the room with his hand in the middle of her back. He told her not to make a fuss, but to be a good girl and sit down next to him. I could feel myself tensing up wondering what would happen if anyone did not obey him.
>
> Dara obediently did as she was told, looking quietly down at the ground. She glanced across at me. As soon as he was no longer looking at her, she quietly slipped off the sofa and out into the passage. I could hear her playing with something, but then a few minutes later it sounded as if something had fallen down. It was followed by whimpering sounds from Dara. Jason looked irritated, raised his voice a little and said, 'For God's sake stop making such a fuss about nothing. You can see I'm busy.' At this I heard Dara run up the stairs.

Question

> What behaviours have you observed Dara to use? How effective are they in relation to meeting her needs? How does this differ in relation to her mother and her father? What insights might this provide in relation to her experience?

COMMENT

There is an interesting contrast between the behaviours that Dara uses with her mother and those that she uses with her father. She uses active behaviours to stay close to her mother. She sometimes smiles and is quiet and conforming, behaving in a socially appealing manner. Her mother responded positively, offering reassurance by smiling back at her and holding out her hand.

With her father, she also tries to be good and conforming, but keeps her distance from him. She tries to minimise her distress and does not seek help when something goes wrong.

Attachment theory: internal working models

We know who we are through the stories (narratives) that we tell ourselves about who we are, about other people and our relationships with them (*I'm generally happy/sad ... I am/am not reasonably good at my job ... People seem not/to like me ... I'm quite friendly and sociable*). These narratives reflect our *internal working models* or the *mental representations* that we carry within us about ourselves, other people and our relationships with them.

Within close relationships, young children develop internal working models of their own worthiness, based on other people's availability and their willingness to give care and protection. In order to function effectively children need to generate internal working models of the self, others and the relationship between the self and others (Howe 1999: 21). By understanding themselves infants begin to make sense of other people and social relationships.

These organised mental representations of the self and others contain expectations and beliefs about:

- *one's own and other people's behaviour*
- *the lovability, worthiness and acceptability of the self*
- *the emotional availability and interest of others, and their ability to provide protection.*

(Howe 1999: 22)

Question

What have you learned so far that might be relevant to understanding Dara's internal working model?

COMMENT

Maria initially responded positively to Dara's expressed need for reassurance in the presence of a stranger. Dara was, however, criticised by her father and he expressed exasperation when she cried. The response from her mother, if reasonably consistent, might enable Dara to develop a view of herself as lovable and effective in gaining a positive response from others, whereas her view of herself in relation to her father may be that she is not lovable and is ineffective in gaining the interest and attention of others. She is therefore trying to be self-reliant.

The internal working model thus determines the characteristic approach used by a person to manage their emotions and ensure that their needs are met. In securely attached people the internal working model carries a confident expectation that disruptions will be resolved (Green 2003: 40). However, where there is less consistency in the response to the infants' attachment-seeking behaviour, the attachment may be less secure. In order to begin to draw any conclusions it would be necessary to observe on a number of occasions, as this behaviour could equally be indicative of an insecure, ambivalent relationship. Research cited by Turney et al (2011) found that social workers had particular difficulties in assessing attachment, with clingy behaviour being seen as evidence of a strong attachment, on the basis of insufficient evidence for any reliable conclusion to be drawn.

Types of attachment

An experimental procedure known as the 'strange situation' was developed by Ainsworth et al (1978) as a way of evaluating the quality of young children's attachment relationships. This entailed observing infants aged 9–18 months from behind a screen in order to see how they reacted when a stranger came into the room in the absence of the main carer (mother), and how they then responded on her return. From this work three categories of attachment were initially identified: secure, insecure ambivalent and insecure avoidant. Subsequently, following work by Main and Solomon (1990) a fourth category has been added, disorganised, which is applied where the child is unable to identify any strategy that has consistent success in ensuring that their needs are met. The descriptions in Howe (1999) are summarised below, showing the relationship between the internal working model and the resulting attachment type.

View of self	View of others	Type of attachment
Loved, effective, autonomous, competent	Available, co-operative, dependable	Secure: in close relationships attachment figures can be relied upon
Unloved, self-reliant	Rejecting, intrusive	Avoidant
Low-value, ineffective, dependant	Neglecting, insensitive, unpredictable, unreliable	Ambivalent
Confused, bad	Frightening, unavailable	Disorganised

Given the significance of attachment as an indicator of emotional development, it is very helpful for practitioners to be aware of indicators that may provide insight into the attachment relationship between a child and her carers. However, it is important that conclusions are not drawn on the basis of single indicators. There are many examples in practice with children and families of *fallible surface Indicators* – '*They were all smiling when I left ... they were all going on a family outing ... the house was clean and tidy*' – being used to infer depth characteristics – '*I thought she loved her ... they seemed to be coping well*' – which are then relied upon to provide reassurance in situations where there is a lack of coherence and reassurance is not justified.

So, if the observer senses that Dara is rather lost, she may draw on attachment theory to seek a *coherent* explanation. The observer had noticed that:

Dara seemed anxious and unable to settle .... She wandered slowly towards the home corner, where there were no other children ... she did not look for any of the staff, but ran back out.

Using attachment theory, these indicators could suggest that Dara does not appear to feel confident about her ability to engage and gain a positive response from either her peers or her substitute carers. This uncertainty could be indicative of an insecure, ambivalent or avoidant attachment to one or both of her parents. It could indicate that her internal working model is of a self that is unlovable and of others who cannot be relied upon to respond positively and meet her needs. The risk when using a coherence strategy is that the practitioner in seeking coherence and meaning continues to notice indicators that fit the pattern, but pays insufficient attention to indicators from other sources that do not fit, or indeed ignores an indicator which simply does not correspond with the pattern that the practitioner is establishing in order to try to come to terms with the mass of uncertain and often contradictory indicators that exist in any real-world practice situation.

Containment

When powerful emotions are received and understood by another person, it allows for growth and development. The containment of pain and learning from experience are central themes in the work of Melanie Klein and Wilfred Bion. According to Klein, a mother who can bear the pain put into her by her child without being overwhelmed acts as a *container* for the feared emotion. If a child finds that her desperate feelings can be accepted and contained by another, she is able at a feeling level to realise that there is someone else capable of doing this and she is then able to gradually learn to do this for herself. Bion (1962) added to the parental function of acting as a container that of a *thinker*: a parent who has a capacity not only to worry and care, but to think about, clarify and differentiate between different kinds of feeling, bringing them together so that the child can make sense of them (Salzberger-Wittenberg et al 1999: 60).

Professionals working with children and families can undertake the role of container, 'containing' feelings so that the client can experience and recognise them (Green 2003).

An example of this is provided in the following observation of Dara, in her reception class at school.

Dara had just arrived and was trying to take off her coat, hat and gloves and hang them on a hook with her name on it. The coat seemed tight and she struggled to pull her arms out. While she was doing this her hat and gloves had fallen on the ground and were then walked on by another child, trying to get to his peg. Dara was frowning and her lips were drawn tightly in. At last (to my relief) she managed to hang up her coat, balance her hat on top of the peg and push the gloves into her pockets. As she turned away to go to her class, the girl using the peg next to her accidentally knocked Dara's clothes off her peg. Dara retrieved her clothes, put them on the little bench under peg and sat on them looking utterly defeated! Thankfully, her efforts had been noticed by the teaching assistant, who walked over to Dara, helping her up and putting her clothes securely on the peg. She bent down and said, 'Dara, I wonder if you might be feeling very fed up. I saw you doing really well hanging up your clothes and then someone knocked them all down.' Dara looked up at her and nodded, but was now happy to go with her into the classroom.

Loss and separation

There are many different situations which may result in social workers needing to observe and work with children who are separated from their primary attachment figures, either permanently or temporarily. Where it is a temporary separation, they often need to observe and understand what is happening when the child is reunited with their attachment figures.

The grief process

As a result of his research Bowlby identified three stages which securely attached children go through when they are separated from carers to whom they are securely attached. These are most evident in children between the ages of six months and four years:

- Initially the child protests vigorously and makes attempts to recover the attachment figure.

- The child despairs about the return of the carer, but continues to be watchful, appearing preoccupied and depressed. When there is a noise at the door the child becomes temporarily alert, hoping that it is the carer returning.

- The child becomes emotionally detached and appears to lose interest in carers in general.

These stages were graphically illustrated in filmed recordings made in the 1950s and 1960s showing the separation behaviour of young children who were previously securely attached (www.robertsonfilms.info). One of the films shows the reunion with his mother of a little boy aged 17 months who had been placed in a residential nursery for nine days while his mother had her second baby. He is seen to cry and struggle away from her, unable to accept her attempts to comfort and hold him. His loss is particularly acute as there is no consistent carer whom he can relate to, his contact with his father is minimal and he has no contact with any extended family.

Many students who have watched this film with me comment that they would previously have assumed that the child was struggling and distressed because he was frightened of his mother and that they would have seen such behaviour as evidence of a poor attachment, rather than the result of a traumatic separation. Children with a strong, close relationship are likely to experience loss and separation as deeply traumatic. An abrupt separation will also exacerbate the distress felt by the child.

This extreme reaction also needs to be understood in the particular cultural context of a small nuclear family, where the child did not appear to have any other close attachment relationships. If, for example, the father is actively involved as an attachment figure, or there is a close extended family network and the child has established attachment relationships with other family members, the impact of the separation may be much less traumatic. Additionally in this example the care environment was completely different: he had moved from a quiet family home with his mother and father to a busy nursery with staff changing in accordance with shift patterns.

The value of understanding that there will be significant reactions by children to separation is that some of what may be observed when children are reunited with their carers reflects the anger and distress that is a *normal* reaction to separation and loss. Children and parents need considerable support to cope with contact sessions which are intrinsically difficult and painful. Unless this is recognised, observers may struggle to understand what they are seeing and run the risk of misconstruing it.

Transference and counter-transference

The concepts of transference and counter-transference are helpful in processing what is happening when we are with other people, particularly in a professional context. The terms were originally developed by Freud and used in psychoanalytic practice.

Transference refers to feelings that one person may unconsciously *transfer* or place on another person. *Counter-transference* refers to the largely unconscious feelings that a worker may have towards a service user, which may mirror those experienced by the service user. Hence the comment by Bion (1990: 5): '*In every consulting room there ought to be two rather frightened people: the patient and the psychoanalyst.*'

Activity

Note down what you noticed about the observer's reactions to Dara's experience. What might this indicate in relation to the observer and in relation to Dara?

COMMENT

Applying this understanding to the encounter between Dara, Maria and the social worker we then need to consider whether:

• Dara is feeling uncertain and frightened and is unconsciously placing those feelings on the social worker (transference);

• the social worker's feelings of uncertainty and uneasiness about Dara mirror the feelings experienced by Dara.

Recognising when transference is happening may be seen as another way of thinking about what is coming from the inside (from the observer) and what is coming from the outside (from those we are observing).

Using research in practice

This final brief section is essentially a plea never to think that research is something that can be seen as separate from practice. This will be illustrated below with reference to the case study about Dara, where research is needed to inform the process of interpretation and reflection and the judgements that may subsequently be made.

The first chapter has hopefully already demonstrated the value of familiarity with research findings by identifying some prevalent themes from child death inquiries which are of immediate relevance to practice. The treatment of these reviews was necessarily selective, focusing on the particular issues of relevance to child observation. However, a wider understanding of what can be learned from them can be gained by reading the overview research reports by Brandon et al commissioned by the Department for Children, Schools and Families (www. dcsf.gov.uk). For example, in the 2005–7 overview report (Brandon et al 2009) of 40 Serious Case Reviews they found that many assessments did not take sufficient account of fathers and men, who tended to be stereotyped as good or bad.

Activity

Thinking about a case you have worked/are working with, how might this finding connect with your practice? How might this be relevant to the observation of Dara?

COMMENT

In the case study of Dara, it is unclear how much is known and understood in relation to Jason. Recognising that a lack of focus on fathers is often a significant issue in understanding a child's experience may encourage practitioners to persevere to ensure that fathers and other men who may be visiting the family home are carefully observed and assessed.

When thinking about Dara, an understanding of the research on the impact of domestic abuse on mothers and children would enable the observer to better understand what she is seeing, as well as think about the most effective ways of working with the family (Cleaver et al 1999; Mullender et al 2002; Humphreys and Stanley 2006; Radford and Hester 2006).

The impact of context

While this book has argued strongly that practice needs to be child centered, it also recognises the relational identities of children (Featherstone et al 2014) and the need to locate any understanding of the child within the context that they live in.

The seminal research by Bebbington and Miles (1989), which highlighted the socio-economic factors that resulted in dramatic differences in the chances of children entering care, is of continuing relevance. The research demonstrates the profound impact of factors such as poverty and overcrowded housing on the experience of children and their families. This needs to be attended to within our observations and reflected on as we attempt to make sense of what we are seeing and consider what intervention may be most helpful.

Activity

Thinking about the family that you identified in the previous activity, what research are you using to inform your work with them?

What else do you need to find out to increase your understanding?

COMMENT

See 'Taking it further', below, for weblinks and some suggestions for further reading.

Conclusion

This chapter has provided some examples of the wide range of theory and research that is relevant to the largely unconscious process of exercising judgement, and to understanding the lives of those who are being observed. It has demonstrated the need to use theoretical constructs and research in order to help practitioners make sense of the uncertainty and complexity with which they are confronted every day. While this can form part of an approach that maximises the use of available evidence, in social work there is rarely sufficient empirical evidence to reach a view or make a judgement based on indicators supported by correspondence with empirical facts. Social workers are thus faced with the need to seek explanations that are coherent. An understanding of relevant research and theory can help us to do this.

Taking it further

Breckon, J and Hay, J (2015) *Knowing How to Protect: Using Research Evidence to Prevent Harm to Children.* London. Alliance for Useful Evidence.

Daniel, B, Wassell, S and Gilligan, R (2010) *Child Development for Child Care and Protection Workers,* 2nd edn. London: Jessica Kingsley.

Howe, D (2005) *Child Abuse and Neglect: Attachment, Development and Intervention,* Basingstoke: Palgrave Macmillan.

http://dartington.org.uk: promotes the use of evidence to improve policy and practice in children's services.

http://dera.ioe.ac.uk/15599/1/assessing_children_in_need_and_their_families_practice_guidance_2000.pdf

www.alliance4usefulevidence.org: forum promoting the use of evidence in decision making.

www.nspcc.org.uk/globalassets/documents/research-reports/knowing-how-to-protect-research-evidence.pdf

www.rcpch.ac.uk/child-health/research-projects/uk-who-growth-charts/. Royal College of Paediatrics and Child Health growth charts

www.rip.org.uk: supports evidence-informed practice with children and families.

References

Ainsworth, M D S, Blehar, M C, Waters, E and Wall, S (1978) *Patterns of Attachment: A Psychological Study of the Strange Situation.* Hillsdale, NJ: Erlbaum.

Bebbington, A and Miles, J (1989) The Background of Children who Enter Local Authority Care. *British Journal of Social Work,* 19(1): 349–68.

Bion, W (1962) *Learning from Experience.* London: Heinemann

Bion, W (1990) *The Brazilian Lectures.* London: Karnac.

Brandon, M, Bailey, S, Belderson, P, Gardner, R, Sidebotham, P, Dodsworth, J, Warren, C and Black, J (2009) *Understanding Serious Case Reviews and their Impact: A Biennial Analysis of Serious Case Reviews 2005–2007,* DCSF-RR129. London: Department for Children, Schools and Families, www.education.gov.uk/publications/standard/ publicationdetail/page1/DCSF-RR129 (accessed 22 September 2015).

Butler, G (2007) Reflecting on Emotion in Social Work, in Knott, C and Scragg, T (eds) *Reflective Practice in Social Work.* Exeter: Learning Matters.

Camus, A (1956) *The Rebel.* New York: Vintage Books.

Cleaver, H, Aldgate, J and Unell, J (1999) *Children's Needs–Parenting Capacity: The Impact of Parental Mental Illness, Problem Alcohol and Drug Use, and Domestic Violence on Children's Development.* London, The Stationary Office.

Daniel, B, Wassell, S and Gilligan, R (2010) *Child Development for Child Care and Protection Workers,* 2nd edn. London: Jessica Kingsley.

Department of Health (2000) *Assessing Children in Need and their Families: Practice Guidance.* London: The Stationery Office, http://dera.ioe.ac.uk/15599/1/assessing_children_in_need_and_their_families_practice_guidance_2000.pdf (accessed 22 September 2015).

Featherstone, B, White, S and Morris, K (2014) *Reimagining Child Protection.* Bristol: Policy Press.

Green, V (2003) *Emotional Development in Psychoanalysis: Attachment Theory and Neuroscience.* Hove: Brunner-Routledge.

Hammond, K R (2007) *Beyond Rationality: The Search for Wisdom in a Troubled Time.* New York: Oxford University Press

Harris, M (2008) *Exploring Developmental Psychology.* London: Sage.

Hart, S (2008) *Brain, Attachment, Personality: An Introduction to Neuroaffective Development.* London: Karnac.

Holmes, J (2001) *The Search for the Secure Base: Attachment Theory and Psychotherapy.* London: Bruner-Routledge.

Howe, D (1999) *Attachment Theory, Child Maltreatment and Family Support: A Practice and Assessment Model.* Basingstoke: Macmillan.

(2005) *Child Abuse and Neglect: Attachment, Development and Intervention*. Basingstoke: Palgrave Macmillan.

Humphreys, C and Stanley, N (2006) *Domestic Violence and Child Protection: Directions for Good Practice*. London: Jessica Kingsley.

Kirkman, E and Melrose, K (2014) *Clinical Judgement and Decision-Making in Children's Social Work: An Analysis of the 'Front Door' System*. London: Department for Education, www.gov.uk/government/uploads/system/uploads/attachment_data/file/305516/RR337_-_Clinical_Judgement_and_Decision-Making_in_Childrens_Social_Work.pdf (accessed 13 August 2015).

Le Riche, P and Tanner, K (1998) *Observation: Its Role and Application in Social Work*. London: Jessica Kingsley.

Main, M and Solomon, J (1990) Procedures for Identifying Infants as Disorganised/Disoriented during the Ainsworth Strange Situation, in Greenberg, M, Cicchetti, D and Cummings, E M (eds) *Attachment during the Preschool Years: Theory, Research and Intervention*. Chicago: University of Chicago Press.

Mullender, A, Hague, G, Imam, U, Kelly, L, Malos, E, and Regan, L (2002) *Children's Perspectives on Domestic Violence*. London: Sage.

Radford, L and Hester, M (2006) *Mothering through Domestic Violence*. London: Jessica Kingsley.

Royal College of Paediatrics and Child Health (RCPCH) (2009) *UK–WHO Growth Charts, 0–18 Years*. London: RCPCH, www.rcpch.ac.uk/improving-child-health/public-health/uk-who-growth-charts/uk-who-growth-charts-0-18-years (accessed 22 September 2015).

Salzberger-Wittenberg, I, Williams, G and Osborne, E (1999) *The Emotional Experience of Learning and Teaching*. London: Karnac.

Thiele, L P (2006) *The Heart of Judgement: Practical Wisdom, Neuroscience, and Narrative*. New York: Cambridge University Press

Turney, D, Platt, D, Selwyn, J and Farmer, E (2011) *Social Work Assessment of Children in Need: What Do We Know?*, DFE-RBX-10-08. Bristol: School for Policy Studies, www.gov.uk/government/uploads/system/uploads/attachment_data/file/182302/DFE-RBX-10-08.pdf (accessed 13 July 2015).

Concluding thoughts

In this book it has been argued that observation, using a holistic, experiential approach, provides a unique opportunity to gain insight into the many paradoxes that comprise the daily, lived experience of children and their families. It is therefore a vital tool for practitioners working with children and families. Developing the skills needed to observe effectively requires time, practice and a disciplined approach, but it is undoubtedly worthwhile.

Key themes emerging from this book include:

*   A recognition that childhood and children are worthwhile: time spent with children is time well spent. Children can share their experience with us if we spend time with them and observe carefully. Wherever children can talk to us, we also need to listen. According to Isaacs (1971: 15): '*By patient listening to the talk of even little children, and watching what they do ... we can wish their wishes, see their pictures and think their thoughts.*'

*   The importance of maintaining an open and 'not knowing' approach, of recognising the limitations and contradictions in what is known and staying with the uncertainty and anxiety that this creates. This was illustrated with reference to Serious Case Reviews, which provide numerous examples of the premature formation of a view about a child's well-being resulting in a subsequent filtering of all information about the child. Being uncertain enables us to remain open to all possibilities.

*   The importance of knowing ourselves, so that we maintain a continual internal dialogue that questions the way in which we are perceiving things, filtering them and interpreting what has been observed. An awareness of the operation of defence mechanisms in this process is essential.

The notion that observing is a very straightforward task has been shown to reveal a woeful lack of understanding, not only of what is required of practitioners working with children and families, but also of the contexts in which the work takes place. In order to move beyond the superficial and see and understand the fine details of children's lives, practitioners need to be courageous, staying with uncertainty and imagining possibilities that do not fit within their own frame of reference. For this to happen there are three preconditions:

1   The availability of professional development and training, ensuring that practitioners can develop skills in observation and maintain their knowledge of theory and current research.

2   A supportive organisational culture that recognises that time spent with children is worthwhile. There is no other way to understand their experience: there are no shortcuts.

3   Effective support and supervision that recognises the painful and stressful elements of practice, so enabling practitioners to be receptive, remain open and process what has been observed.

Given the call by Munro (2011) for a rebalancing of priorities in social work, between bureaucratic and professional requirements, it could be argued that it is incumbent upon organisations to find ways of enabling this shift to take place, which would help to ensure that these preconditions are addressed and that practitioners are able to be effective. For, despite the difficult climate in which work with children and their families takes place and the often demanding nature of the work, especially in child protection contexts, practice that is centred on understanding and supporting children and their families can also be a uniquely valuable, rich, rewarding and positive experience that makes a great difference to the well-being of children and their families. However, it is important to acknowledge that even where the preconditions listed above are addressed, there will still be limitations in some practice contexts, which will mean that even the most skilful practitioners will not necessarily be aware of some of the distress that has been carefully concealed from view. In such situations it is helpful to be secure in the knowledge that you have taken every step possible to develop your skills and safeguard the child's well-being.

References

Isaacs, S (1971) *The Nursery Years: The Mind of the Child from Birth to Six Years*. London: Routledge.

Munro, E (2011) *The Munro Review of Child Protection: Final Report. A Child-Centred System*, Cm 8062. London: The Stationery Office.

Index